FOLKLORE AND CUSTOMS
OF
RURAL ENGLAND

FOLKLORE AND CUSTOMS
OF
RURAL ENGLAND

Margaret Baker

DAVID & CHARLES
NEWTON ABBOT   LONDON

ROWMAN & LITTLEFIELD
TOTOWA, NEW JERSEY

This edition first published in 1974
in Great Britain by
David & Charles (Publishers) Ltd
Newton Abbot Devon
in the U.S.A. by
Rowman & Littlefield
Totowa New Jersey

0 7153 6579 7 *(Great Britain)*

Library of Congress Cataloging in Publication Data

Baker, Margaret, 1928–
  Folklore and customs of rural England.

  Bibliography: p.
  1. England—Social life and customs. 2. Country life—England.
3. Folk-lore—England.   I. Title.
DA110.B26   390'.0942   74-7065
ISBN 0-87471-549-0

Printed in Great Britain
by Redwood Burn Limited Trowbridge & Esher

Contents

List of Illustrations

List of Illustrations

Introduction

Only within the last fifty years have customs and folklore ceased to be everyday forces in rural life. Once they governed the smallest act in home, farm and village, giving rules and rituals for the proper performance of tasks, the safeguarding of family, farm and possessions, reflecting the natural longing of individual and community alike for prosperity, happiness and security.

Men spent their lives watching the plough transform the soil, the springing wheat which followed and, at the end, the richness of harvest. Work and pleasure joined hands in perfect amity in the customary pastoral feasts. 'Fifty year ago 'twere all mirth and jollity,' said an old Gloucestershire labourer about 1898, with retrospective generosity. 'There was four feasts in the year for us folks. First of all there was the sowers' feast—that would be about the end of April; then came the sheep-shearers' feast—there'd be about fifteen of us as would sit down after sheep-shearing, and we'd be singing best part of the night, and plenty to eat and drink; next came the feast for the reapers, when the corn was cut about August; and, last of all, the harvest home in September. Ah, those were good times fifty years ago.'[1] And this was echoed in nineteenth-century Devon where, for a farmer's family: 'There was plenty of work but also plenty of fun, for families were large. The long working hours of summer were broken by flower shows, club walks and fairs. In winter parties were numerous. Cards, party games and dancing were the amusements . . . a party began in the afternoon, for long distances had to be travelled by many of the guests, either by trap or on horseback, girls sometimes riding pillion.'[2]

Dark superstitions and customs (often remnants of atavistic cultures, taboos and religions long forgotten in their own rights) were widely found up to the late nineteenth century, although long before that some had come gently to mock them. About 1700 Henri Misson de Valbourg, a French visitor to England, had asked a number of people why they nailed horseshoes to their thresholds and had received varied answers, although it was generally held to keep witches away. 'It is true they laugh when they say this,' he wrote, 'but yet they do not laugh at it altogether; for they believe there is, or at least may be, some secret virtue concealed in it'³—a frame of mind not unknown today. But whether there were always some to laugh at them or not, the old practices had a firm grip. Today it is hard to comprehend how pervasive they were; a hundred charms provided for birth, marriage and death, preparing a field, churning butter, beekeeping, baking and brewing. Country cures and medicines were general; wisewomen looked into the future and dealt effectively with evil-wishers; the country calendar with its dancing, plays and rituals welded the tightly knit community in a common social pattern.

As late as 1898 Richard Blakeborough wrote of Yorkshire: 'Many of the dales are far removed from the varied influences of the outer world; they are self-contained communities. Some of the old folk have never seen a locomotive. It is in such places that the student may gather a rich harvest of folklore.'⁴ This lore formed part of the secret folklife of the countryside, part of its driving force, not cherished from antiquarian affection or regarded as something rarified or arcane, but as the collective and immensely valuable wisdom of the community, constantly employed in everyday activity.

The fabric of the old rural society was enduring but changes began to come at last. The Industrial Revolution began the break-up of the old ways of thought. Railways brought cheap and easy travel to a people once dependent upon horse and carrier's cart; no longer were country people confined, often for a lifetime, to one group of villages, one market town, or a solitary northern valley. The Education Acts of 1870 and 1902 made literacy a commonplace, with an accompanying demand for books, newspapers and postal services and a broadening of experience. The enclosure movement and farm mechanisation from the eighteenth century onwards, and the decline in British agriculture from about 1875 with the consequent reduction in the agricultural labour force, made country folk look outside their villages for employment and the drift to the towns was steady.

Farming science had developed under the agricultural societies and progressive landlords, and rational explanations were offered for former mysteries, amending husbandry practices which had changed little since the days of the Elizabethan farmers and in some instances—the use of sickle and flail for example—from prehistoric times. Except on hill-farms horses and oxen were no longer necessarily the major motive-force of the farm and the primeval indispensability of horse-keepers and blacksmiths suffered its first setback. Victorian radicality of thought at least partially loosened the hold of church and parson and from about 1900 onwards the gradual disintegration of the great estates, with their near-feudal administration, began.

As the twentieth century advanced the inexorable pattern continued; the first country buses and cars appeared, destroying the old attachment to place; teachers with unfamiliar accents and fresh ideas took over the village schools; two world wars brought forced population movements and the arrival of telephone, radio and television completed the release of the village from its former social isolation. Despite a tendency among countrymen to paint a rosier picture of the 'good old days' than the facts sustain, there was generally little regret for the passing of a period of unremitting labour, poverty and hunger for so many in the village community. 'Times be better now, and a good thing they be,' said William Plastow aged 87 in 1927.[5]

In the demarcation of the old rural world from the new, dates are significant; in general and in both England and North America, 1914 marked the division between these two very different cultures. The ending of an era was characterised by poignant *vales*. Pencilled on the whitewashed beam of a barn at Peasmarsh, Sussex, were a cowman's homely reminders—'Strawberry went to the Bull March 10th '06'; 'Finished Harvest Sept. 10th' and a last entry, 'Went to the War August 25th 1914'. World War I consolidated changes which, although felt earlier, had so far left the true foundations of rural life untouched. Only those who had lived their adolescence or mature years before 1914 fully experienced the abundance of old lore at work in the community; the next generation was to fall under the disruptive in-

Introduction

fluences of post-war cynicism; its temper changed and its thoughts were all of reappraisal, question and rejection. Yet there is no ultimate agreement as to dates. For example Walter Rose, village builder of Haddenham, was inclined to feel that it was being born as early as 1871 that gave him knowledge of the old world and the new; it was early enough, he said, for him to catch the last of the old life then rapidly passing away, yet late enough for him to witness the coming of the new.[6]

Whatever the critical date, no longer would the innocent pleasures of riding for the ribbon at weddings, divination on St Mark's Eve, telling the bees of family happenings, harvest-homes, club walks, fairs, sheep-shearings and Christmas provide excitement enough to last the whole year through. Over the century, people had inevitably become less parochial, less credulous, less ready to accept their fathers' life-style and as soon as the old beliefs and amusements were seen as foolish and unsophisticated, their fate was certain.

But while changing life-patterns were eroding their influence in England, the old ways were carried to America and Canada with the great waves of nineteenth-century emigration and under the spartan stimulus of pioneer conditions were sometimes given fresh life, when they were coming to be forgotten at home. The merry barn-raisings, sociable bees, weddings and wakes, the settlers' lore of field and cow-shed, were sustained both by the plain necessity for communal action merely to survive in isolation, and by an eager grasping—in the absence of material resources—at all support, whether of superstitious origin or not. Nothing was more natural, after all, than that settlers should draw reassurance in their new life from preservation of the ways of the old.

Today it would be ill-advised and hasty to dismiss the old lore as totally dead. Many irrational beliefs are no longer overt, but they linger, embodied in subconscious folk memory, more stoutly rooted than we know. Hints of tenacity are found in country conversations ('No harm in trying it . . . My mother always said . . .'). Older Devonians are still reluctant to wash blankets in May, jam is stirred sunwise, Buckinghamshire beans are sown on Ashendon Feast Day, and apple trees are wassailled, even in the glare of television

12

lights. As long as man's essential nature remains, with its hopes and fears, its emotional irrationality and its accompanying beliefs and precautionary procedures, these practices seem likely to survive.

England and America are still at heart, and in their private and fondest estimations, rural countries. Few families cannot look back to some link with the nineteenth- or early twentieth-century countryside, to a country aunt or grandmother visited in childhood perhaps, or to family stories of rural trades or farming ancestors. In a typical migration pattern the writer's paternal grandfather, son of a Bramley sawyer, and grandmother, child of farm labourers at Peasemore, Berkshire, were drawn upon their marriage in 1874 to the prosperous railway and biscuit town of Reading, but they never forgot their rural lore and passed it on to their children. Phil Drabble, the Staffordshire writer, recalls that he, son of a Black Country doctor, learned his country lore from miners and ironworkers, three or four generations removed from those who had flocked from the countryside at the Industrial Revolution, but remaining superstitious countrymen, excellent stock-keepers, keenly interested in gardening, ferreting, mushrooming, and other country pursuits.[7] There are many families on both sides of the Atlantic and elsewhere to whom the lore of this book will speak, even if only in faint and half-remembered voice.

Clearly it would be impossible, with any hope of including even a tithe of significant material, to compress the great body of country beliefs and practices into a short book for general reading. Gathering eligible facts and instances proved only too easy and the inevitable cutting painful. But even with omissions, of which the author is very aware, it is hoped that the more important beliefs and customs which give perspective and clarity to country life have at least received some attention, with an indication of the way in which they crossed the Atlantic with settlers moving to new lands. Contemporary accounts have been included where possible, for present beliefs form the surest point from which to take a backward glance, with enough historical material to show the richness of what now inevitably lies behind us, often within living memory, but never again to be experienced at first hand in the rural community.

1

On the Farm:
Fields and Fertility

Until the development of scientific agriculture (largely within the last hundred years) the farmer had little but the accumulated lore of past centuries, strengthened by practical experience, to sustain him in the face of nature's uncertainties. Farming lore falls into two main classes: the first of magical, irrational origin, appeasing unknown forces, and the second based on close observation of weather and natural circumstances affecting husbandry. Sometimes the two seem inextricably confused, but drawing from one or the other the farmer could confirm his role as activator between nature and land. He would be told how to sow, to increase his fields' fertility, to protect his stock from evil. The all-important corn-harvest had distinctive ceremonies all its own.

Mechanisation and science struck the old lore a blow but the new thought was not, of course, immediately acceptable to all; one old farmer, emerging from an agricultural lecture as recently as thirty years ago, was heard to say: 'A bit of scientific's all right. But it don't take much of it to ruin a decent farm.' Research has confirmed the validity of some beliefs; the Herefordshire conviction, for example (apparently derived from the apple's magical reputation), that a hop-yard planted in an orchard's stead would fail, now seems based on a sound knowledge of plant affinities, whether superstitiously acquired or not.

MAGIC AND THE FIELDS

Ancient magic secured the farm's fertility. In Worcestershire, Hereford-shire and Gloucestershire, twelve Twelfth Night fires leaping and dancing in hopeful simulation of waving grain, were lighted in the wheat fields and round a thirteenth, larger, fire the farmer, servants and friends gathered in the winter dark to drink a cheerful, hallooing toast in warm cider to the next harvest, and to eat rich plumcake as an earnest of plenty. The party then went to supper and later to the cowshed carrying a special cake with a hole in it.

> Fill your cups, my merry men all!
> For here's the best ox in the stall,
> Oh! He is the best ox, of that there's no mistake
> And so let us crown him with the Twelfth cake,

was the toast, and the ox was encouraged to toss his head and throw the cake into the air. If it fell before him, it belonged to the bailiff, if behind to the mistress. Round every village Twelfth Night fires burned in the bare fields, twinkling away into the night as far as the eye could see, while answering shouts and halloos marked other celebrations; the ritual was enduring, for even in 1898 it was still the custom to bring the cow into the farmyard in Herefordshire and to put the cake upon her horn.[1]

On New Year's morning until at least 1913 in the West Midlands, farm-women plaited a new hawthorn globe as a fire and fertility charm to be baked in the oven and hung in the kitchen until the following year. While they worked, the men, 'burning the bush', fired the old globe in the field and carried it flaring over the first-sown wheat, smouldering twigs falling into every furrow. One observer wrote censoriously that the workers sang 'Old Cider' during the burning and that it was common to see 'labouring men early on New Year's morning in a beastly state of drunkenness arising from this foolish custom'.[2] On 31 December 1877, Parson Kilvert of Bred-wardine heard the merry New Year peal of bells and from his bed saw the fires springing up everywhere to bathe the valley in flickering light.[3]

Farmers encouraged luck-bringing rooks to build in their trees, for 'rooks only build where there's money'. About 1942 a Middlesex man spoke at Harrow Weald of his uncle who had farmed there without much success. There were no rooks on the farm so he paid young men to climb his trees carrying bags of twigs to build artificial nests in the hope of attracting the birds, but they did not come. Genuine nests from neighbouring rookeries were next tried but their owners did not follow. The farmer then changed farms and moved to Sheepcote Road, Harrow; the very next year rooks built on the farm, his grassland proved to be excellent 'early bite' and later the turf and then the land were sold profitably as developers moved into the district about 1900—all attributed to the beneficial presence of the rooks.[4]

A rookery on the farm brought prosperity

PLOUGHING AND THE SOIL

Soil was a source of lore. Land where a crime had been committed was eternally sterile and poor fields earned wry nicknames: Empty Purse, Bare Bones, Pinchgut, Labour-in-Vain: one sour covert at Shinfield, Berkshire was aptly called The Devil's Garden. But good land was praised: Pound of Butter, Fillpockets, Land of Promise, New Delight or Dripping Pan.[5] East Anglian farmers, weary of never-ending stone-picking, believed within living memory that stones bred spontaneously from pudding-stone or conglomerate, called mother, quick or breeding-stone. Ploughmen were in special communion with the soil. Frank Williams in *Sussex Notes and Queries*,

August 1944, wrote that in 1924 near Harting, he had seen an old ploughman drop a piece of his 'plum heavy' elevenses cake into a furrow for luck, a practice common in Normandy but less so in Sussex. Yorkshire and Suffolk farmers never began ploughing on Friday when soil must not be disturbed with iron tools—blending ancient reverence for iron with the Christian significance of Friday, a poor day for new agricultural activity: for the first lamb to be dropped, for churning, for sowing or reaping to begin, for the last load of harvest. Farmers might start work on Thursday night to avoid the stigma.

Marling, spreading a fine-grain clay soil including carbonate of lime, now remembered only by the field name Marlpit, was a general procedure until about 1870. Squire Nicholas Blundell wrote in July 1712 of his estate near Liverpool: 'I had my Finishing Day for my Marling and abundance of my Neighbours and Tennants eat and drink with me in ye Afternoon, Several of them had made presents to my wife of Sugar, Chickens, Butter etc: All my Marlers, spreaders, water-balys and carters dined here. We fetched home ye Maypowl from the Pit and had Sword dansing and a Mery night in ye Hall and in ye Barne.'[6]

Plough Days or 'throng work', echoed by the bees of pioneer North America, were friendly occasions when neighbours loaned ploughs, horses and ploughmen to help a farmer newly moved to his farm. In 1808 a Guisborough, Yorkshire, farmer's wife made these preparations for a plough day on her farm, attended by the formidable number of eighty ploughs. Twelve bushels of wheat were ground for 17 white loaves and 51 dumplings, with 42 pounds of currants and 14 pounds of raisins, for which 7 pounds of sugar, vinegar and butter made the sauce. One hundred and ninety-six pounds of beef and more followed, 2 large hams and 4 pounds of peasepudding, 3 Cheshire cheeses and 2 twenty-eight pound homemade cheeses. Ninety-nine gallons of ale and 2 of rum rounded off the hearty feast. In 1850 an Oxfordshire squire, John Whitmore, of Chastleton House, had a farm unexpectedly left on his hands at a tenant's death. His neighbours proposed a 'love-hawl'; he had but to provide beer, cheese and seed-corn, and the neighbours would help. Whitmore expected a few ploughs but to his amazement sixty-eight teams appeared, decked with ribbons out of respect for the squire.[7]

The ploughing-match is an agricultural custom which has triumphantly survived mechanisation. Matches, often including horse-ploughing classes, are held all over England and North America by old or regenerated custom. In 1971 Nova Scotia revived its annual match for heavy horses and ten teams competed. In the same year the Southern Counties Horse Ploughing Association was formed in England to foster interest in the older method of ploughing.[8] Pulling or drawing matches, tests of strength for oxen or horses, once occasions for wagers in East Anglia, are still popular at many North American fall fairs.

SOWING THE SEED

Seed is important for both symbolic and intrinsic reasons, a link between hope and fulfilment for the farmer. Superstition governed sowing. From Norfolk to Nova Scotia and Kentucky, labourers believed that should a seed-drill 'miss a bout' and go from one end of the field to the other without depositing seed, someone connected with the farm would die before reaping. One writer told how, about 1830, when an elderly relative of his died in Berkshire, the farm overseer sagely remarked that he had missed seeding a row, which was then pointed out in the wheatfield. 'Who could disbelieve it now?' asked the old man. This old superstition was carried forward from the days of hand-sowing and indeed may not be dead in its earlier form. In 1939 on Manor Farm, Brightling, Sussex, when a seed-drill had broken down, the writer helped the farm bailiff, Henry Whiteman, to sow a field by hand. Sacks of wheat were placed at intervals along the headland and the flat basket or seedcote, hanging by a leathern strap round the sower's neck, was refilled at the end of the rows, marked by peeled white sticks from the hedge. The old belief was mentioned. 'Mustn't miss a row, or we'll lose one of the family.'

Farmers chose sowing days carefully. Saints' days were favourable: 'St Valentine, set thy hopper by mine, St Mattho, take thy hopper and sow.' East Anglian farmers, making a fundamental test of the soil's readiness in a fragment of an ancient fertility ritual, took off their trousers and sat on the tilth to test its readiness for planting. Hundreds of cultivation rhymes guided the farmer, governing every crop and varying according to district, climate or personal fancy. Typical was:

> When the elm leaf is as big as a mouse's ear
> Then to sow barley, never fear.

Budding leaves were a planting guide in many agricultures, and settlers in America were advised by the Indians that only when whiteoak, elm and hickory leaves in the hills, and osage orange leaves on the plains, were the size of squirrels' ears, was it safe to plant corn. In Somerset and Devon oat-sowing was linked to the church's year. 'My man, bred on the border of Exmoor,' wrote J. M. Hawker in 1883, 'said to me one day, "When the parson begins to read Genesis, it's time to sow black oats." '[9]

Thomas Tusser, Elizabethan farmer at Cattawade on the Stour estuary, prolific adviser in rhyme on agricultural matters and a shrewd employer who understood inducements, spoke of the sower's traditional rewards:

> Wife, sometime this week, if the weather hold clear,
> An end of wheat-sowing we make for the year.
> Remember you, therefore, though I do it not,
> The seedcake, the pasties and frumentie pot.

At Blunham, Bedfordshire, in the nineteenth century, the completion of wheat-sowing was marked by the farmers' wives with neighbourly gifts to friends of sweet dough and caraway-seed 'siblett' cakes; a villager told William Hone that one season she had been surprised to receive fifteen such cakes.[10]

In both England and North America the moon, emblem of increase, dying, and being reborn three days later, is still thought to influence seeds and growth of all kinds; a view with some scientific support, for the moon's faint glow links daylight growing hours and growth processes may therefore continue at a very low level during the night. In general it is said that seeds sown or grafts made with the waxing moon will grow with her, but beliefs often appear contradictory and are seldom explicit. Some advise that seeds be sown during the new moon itself; others favour the last days of the wane so that germinated seeds may grow with the waxing moon. Tusser, expressing Suffolk sentiments plainly enough, wrote:

> Sow pease (good Trull),
> The moon past full,
> Fine seeds then sow,
> Whilst moon doth grow.

And

> Sow peasen and beans in the wane of the moon,
> Who soweth them sooner, he soweth too soon,
> That they with the planet may rest and arise,
> And flourish with bearing most plentiful wise,

—advice consolidated in the cryptic Suffolk saying 'February wane, peas and bane' [beans]. 'Never fell by moonlight' was an axiom obeyed until at least 1900; cutting and harvesting crops and herbs, and timber-felling for wood to be seasoned, must be done at the moon's dark, for mature substances continued growth and moved naturally towards rot, in moonlight. But 'fell frith, coppice and fuel at the first quarter' counselled *The Husbandman's Practice or Prognostication for Ever*, 1664, since brushwood cut at the waxing would increase in bulk.

'One to rot and one to grow, one for the pigeon, one for the crow' was the sower's rule. Predators stole the seed and small boys with clappers guarded fields, shouting:

> Away, away, away, birds
> Take a little bit and come another day, birds,
> Great birds, little birds, pigeons and crows
> I'll up with my clappers and down she goes![11]

The Bridewell Museum, Norwich, has an evocative birdscarer's clapper with the rough outline of a bird carved upon it.

WEATHER

Although occasionally beneficial—'A wet May makes big loads of hay'—bad weather is generally damaging to the comfort and prosperity of the rural community. Those knowledgeable in weather patterns are still heeded, although their role has inevitably diminished with the growth of scientific weather forecasting. The long view is important:

> Onion skin very thin,
> Mild winter coming in,
> Onion skin thick and tough,
> Coming winter cold and rough,

said shrewd gardeners, and key days governed forecasting:

> If Candlemas Day be fair and bright,
> Winter will have another flight,
> If Candlemas Day be clouds and rain,
> Winter be gone and will not come again.

In North America, should the groundhog see his own shadow on 2 February, winter is only half done, an old prediction upon which every newspaper comments. English farmers, agreeing that winter might still have teeth in February, said:

> A farmer should, on Candlemas Day,
> Have half his corn and half his hay,

but:

> On Candlemas Day if the thorns hang adrop,
> You can be sure of a good pea crop.

Signs portended rain:

> If the bees stay at home,
> Rain will soon come;
> If they fly away,
> Fine will be the day.

Arthur Randell's father always visited the beehives before planning his day's work out of doors. One of the most-quoted weather rhymes notices leafing sequences:

> If the oak's before the ash,
> You will only get a splash,
> But if the ash precedes the oak,
> You will surely get a soak.

22

More economically, 'Oak choke, ash splash'. Another spring sign was:

> Rain on Good Friday or Easter Day,
> A good crop of grass but a bad one of hay.

An adage whose truth, it was said, had been amply proved. A West Country ploughmen's rhyme, based on Bristol Channel tides, ran:

> If it raineth when it doth flow,
> Then yoke your ox and go to plough.
> But if it raineth when it doth ebb,
> Unyoke your ox and goe to bed.

Across the Atlantic this became:

> Raining on the flood,
> Nothing but a scud [shower],
> Raining on the ebb,
> Might as well go to bed.[12]

Farsighted Fenland labourers struck ploughs with an iron hammer; a dull note portended rain, but a high, clear note coming snow and

> If the moon shows a silver shield,
> Be not afraid to reap your field,
> But if she rises haloed round,
> Soon we'll tread on deluged ground,

said harvestmen, pressing ahead with their work.

'We've had a lot of rain, Harry', Cecil Atkins of Waddesdon remembers saying to Harry Dormer of Upper Winchendon. 'I know'd we should,' said Harry. 'Saturday moon and Sunday full, Allus brings rain and allus 'ull', for the moon is as closely aligned with weather as with sowing. 'The moon and the weather change together' is a prediction as likely to be heard in New England as in Devon.

Old names for sun, moon and stars lingered late in rural usage. Miss Nancy Quayle writes (1973) that on an April day about 1921 she was working in the nine-acre field at Brantham, Suffolk, with an old countryman, Stephen Rout—'Old Stivvy'. 'He kept looking up, saying, " 'Ere come Phoebe". I looked round for one of his granddaughters, but saw no one. Finally I realised that he said it when the sun—Phoebus Apollo—broke through the clouds.' The old classical name used by Shakespeare and later poets survived in this form in the old country-inn songs. Until he was taken to London by Miss Quayle's family, 'Old Stivvy', who could neither read nor write had never been outside Suffolk and had a rich store of Shakespearian turns of phrase: 'That's too late to plant that. Toime that comes the fearsome heat o' the sun that'll whoolly burn', reminiscent of:

> Fear no more the heat o' the sun,
> Nor the furious winter's rages ...
> *Cymbeline.* Act 4, scene 2, 258.

Iron would not weld, blacksmiths said, when lightning was near, although after a storm they carefully refilled cooling troughs with storm water, thought particularly effective for tempering iron. Safe places of shelter during thunderstorms were hawthorn trees, or, in accord with the animal's strength and invincibility, a bull's pen, where lightning would never strike.

A village rhyme, well known in eighteenth-century Bedfordshire (all the names are still to be found in the county today) spoke of a man named Duncombe, of Houghton Regis, a dealer in Dunstable larks—and of the eternal difficulties of reliable weather prediction:

> Well, Duncombe, how will be the weather?
> Sir—it looks cloudy altogether.
> And coming across our Houghton Green
> I stopped and talked with old Frank Beane.
> While we stood there, sir, old Jan Swain
> Went by, and said he knowed 'twould rain.
> The next that came was Master Hunt,
> And he declared he knew it wouldn't.
> And then I met with Father Blow,
> He plainly said he didn't know.
> So sir, when doctors disagree,
> Who's to decide it, you or me?

WEEDS

Weeds, perennial enemies, were superstitiously thought to arise from the very soil itself and not necessarily from parent plants, a comforting rationalisation of infestation offered in Suffolk as late as 1887. Efforts to eradicate weeds would surely fail and were indeed almost impious, for the soil was cursed at Adam's fall and would always bear weeds for the farmer's punishment. Husbandmen had eloquent names for the greatest scourges: hellweed, strangle tare, scaldweed or devil's guts for dodder: ropebind, jack-run-in-the-country and devil's garters for convolvulus; ground glutton for groundsel. Sir Thomas Browne (1605-82), the Norwich doctor and antiquary, saw Norfolk farmers place chalked tile charms at corners and middles of fields, against dodder and tetter (the common celandine). Future growth of weeds was *not* desired, so it was politic to pull them at the moon's wane and before Midsummer Day. In Herefordshire a contest cheered the dreary Easter task of 'corn-showing', weeding the corncockle from the 'Lent grain' or spring wheat; he who pulled the first plant or the most, received the largest piece of cake at the field feast, or a kiss from the prettiest girl present. Although the custom faded about 1880 it was affectionately remembered by old men in the Golden Valley as late as 1912.[13]

HARVEST-TIME

The fragrant hay-harvest, first of the year's ingathering, began about 11 June ('By St Barnabas put scythe to the grass') and went on into July; in the Fens scythes were 'July razors'. Their use continued late. Walter Rose of Haddenham, born in 1871, remembered that while horse-drawn mowers had appeared there in his boyhood, the scythe was still used for fields of unusual shape or contour.[14] Hayfield democracy was universal. Parson Kilvert wrote in his diary on Midsummer Eve 1875, of a long day working in the meadows alongside the haymakers, finishing in the warm shadows of a sweet-smelling Wiltshire dusk.

With all harvesting the industrious were valued; 'Two good haymakers are worth twenty crackers', or boasters, said farmers.[15] The elaborate ceremonies of corn-harvest were usually absent, but an extra jar of ale was brought out and the men sat down for a chat with perhaps a song or two and a cheer at the day's end.

Between haysel and grain harvest comes a brief lull (often the time for agricultural shows); then the casual workers who came to Cambridgeshire farms shyly announced their arrival by scraping their scythes on the farm's cobbled yard. When hiring was done, each received a shilling *handsel* and a pint of beer, recalled Mr K. Tebbitt of Orchard Farm, Toft, in 1962. In Lancashire, where Sunday hiring was usually frowned upon, four Sundays in harvest were free of restriction, although there was no latitude about field-work then. William Henry Edwards remembered hearing of the tenant of Jackson's Fen, Huntingdonshire, who about 1865 harvested on Sunday and could do nothing with his land afterwards. 'Justly rewarded' was the village verdict.[16] Regular workers struck a special harvest bargain with the farmer through their chosen 'lord', who spoke for them and shook the farmer's hand on their behalf when matters were settled. Negotiations sometimes went on for half the day before 'dewbeer', to wet the sickle and drink success to harvest, was sent for. The contract was no small matter, for thirty reapers might be needed in one field, each taking eleven rows of corn upon his blade at a single cut and each followed by his sheaver, 'John Grout', a retired Suffolk farmer of 88, remembered about 1967. His long-lived father and grandfather had worked the same 150 acre farm so he was in touch with eighteenth-century farming.[17]

The harvest-lord (still chosen in Essex in 1923),[18] sober and industrious with red poppies and green bindweed round his rush hat as badge of office, set the working pace, was always respectfully addressed as 'my lord' and was served first at mealtimes. He superintended the yellow stoneware jar of cool ale hidden in the hedge leaves, 'shod' new reapers in return for beer in the field, and later presided over the harvest-home feast.

Anyone trampling the corn and making it harder to cut was fined by the lord who used the money for 'trailing beer' (one careless Suffolk farmer's wife paid for allowing her hens into uncut corn), and a stranger passing the field would be asked for a shilling for beer under the old custom of 'crying largesse', which survived in Suffolk into the nineteenth century. Thomas Tusser advised the farmer:

Grant, harvest-lord, more by a penny or two,
To call on his fellowes, the better to do;
Give gloves to thy reapers a largess to crie,
And daily to loiterers have a good eie.

Gloves were a customary gift to reapers, especially if the wheat
was thistly, and as late as 1914 glove money of 2s 6d appeared on the
harvest wages bill. Music of hone against blade rang out from barns
and wild-arum or mouse-ear juice was rubbed along each blade as a
charm to keep it sharp through harvest. Harvesters' days were long;
the tin horn was blown at dawn at the farmhouse door (old William
King of Melbourn, Cambridgeshire, who died in 1935 at the age of
84, had blown the harvest-horn from the age of seven), and to quench
enormous thirsts in dusty fields, seventeen pints of beer were allowed
each man every day, said 'John Grout'. The farmer for whom Arthur
Randell worked as a boy about 1910 was an even more spectacular
drinker, and Mr Randell remembers being sent three times a day
to the Galloping Donkey to fetch eight bottles of beer in a sack;
the farmer would down a bottle in a gulp or two, then with a cheerful
shout to his horse, get on with the work. Although he could drink
as many as thirty pints in a harvest-day, he was never known to be
drunk.

The corn-harvest, crown of the farming year, engendered varied
emotions; anxiety lest the weather fail, tension during the work itself,
and half-fearful joy at the ritual capture of the corn-spirit, upon
whose favour a full rickyard depended. The farmer shared these
sentiments with his men. The farm's prosperity belonged to all and the
satisfaction at work accomplished through mutual effort was sociably
expressed later at the homely harvest-feast. At harvest-time labourers
moved outside their workaday selves, beyond the ordinary dimensions
of their lives. They could both demand favours and receive them,
the established pattern of master and man was forgotten and in the
glare of the late summer sun all men stood equal in the field, securely
bound in common purpose to antique and satisfying roles. Robert
Herrick struck the true note of harvest in 'The Hock-cart, or Harvest-
Home':

Come Sons of Summer, by whose toile,
We are the Lords of Wine and Oile:
By whose tough labours, and rough hands,
We rip up first, then reap our lands.
Crown'd with the eares of corne, now come,
And, to the Pipe, sing Harvest home . . .[19]

Customs varied from one county to the next but were essentially
the age-old rites of harvest. Even in the railway age, farm labourers
stood, hats in hand, sunburned and weary, amid the golden sheaves,
following ceremonies which would have been familiar to harvesters
in the ancient fields of Greece and Egypt. They worked in a steadily
decreasing circle until only the final ears, in which the prepotent
corn-spirit was hiding, remained uncut. There was a superstitious
reluctance to sever them; sometimes the reapers threw sickles from a
safe distance, then none was branded as the spirit's captor. The moment,
full of ritual meaning, was called 'crying the neck', 'knack' or
'mare'.

The last stalks were worked into the mysterious figure of the corn-
or kern-dolly, baby, maiden, or ivy-girl (dressed by Kentish women
in paper cut like finest lace), and kept at the farm, emblematic of the
continuity of seasons. Corn-dollies in traditional shapes—Durham
chandelier, Northamptonshire horns and Suffolk horseshoe—are now
sophisticated craft objects, but witch-repellent red thread still ties
them and protective magic lingers.[20] An old man who visited Cambridge Folk Museum in recent years knew of the true corn-dolly-
making from his grandmother who lived at Litlington and who died
in 1903 aged 75. There, until about 1848, she said, after the harvest
feast at which the final plaiting of the dolly was done and it was given
a special chair, the farmer, accompanied only by the farm-men,
carried it carefully to the parlour and put it away on the top of the
corner cupboard to rest safely until the next summer. As an awe-
struck child, she remembered creeping in to peer at the dolly lying
limply there, guardian of the next harvest. Each year for over one
hundred years, a family at Whalton, Northumberland, has made a
kern-baby, the height of a sheaf of corn, which is left in the church
until the following year. Mrs Ridley, a recent maker of the baby,

and her sister, well remember their mother and grandmother doing the work.[21]

In July 1826 a gentleman farmer sent William Hone a luminous account of 'crying the neck' in his North Devon fields. In the last field reaped the oldest reaper or another knowledgeable in the ceremony collected the best ears among the sheaves, plaiting the straw 'very tastefully' into the device of the neck. Reapers, binders and women clustered round the man who held it; he stooped low and held it near the ground while the men also bent to the stubble, pulling off their hats. Slowly, with a long musical cry of 'The neck' repeated thrice, they rose. Hats flew into the air, girls were kissed and the reaper who could snatch the neck ran as hard as he could to the farmhouse where the dairymaid stood waiting with a pail of water. If he could enter the house unseen he might lawfully kiss her—otherwise he was 'regularly soused'.

'On a fine, still autumn evening,' continued Hone's correspondent, 'the crying of the neck has a wonderful effect at a distance . . . I have once or twice heard upwards of twenty men cry it, and sometimes joined by an equal number of female voices. About three years back on some high grounds, where our people were harvesting, I heard six or seven 'necks' cried in one night, although I know that some of them were four miles off. They are heard through the quiet evening air, at a considerable distance sometimes. But I think that the practice is beginning to decline of late, and many farmers and their men do not care about keeping up this old custom. I shall always patronise it myself, because I take it in the light of a thanksgiving.'

In Hertfordshire it was 'crying the mare'. Three times the reaper of the last sheaf called 'I have her' and his fellows responded 'What have you?' 'A mare, a mare, a mare!' 'Whose is she?' 'Mister Thomas Puddephat's' (their master). 'Where will you send her?' 'To Mr John Snooks!' (another farmer, tardier with harvest). Then staid horses were set galloping like colts (gateposts were knocked down and waggons overturned in the urgency of harvest), and the reapers chased the last leaf-strewn 'horkey' load with bowls of water to throw over the sheaves while the village women smiled and waved from their open doors. The beaming farmer's wife and her daughters

stood waiting with jugs of beer as the last precious load swung into
the yard to the triumphant cry:

> We have ploughed, we have sowed,
> We have reaped, we have mowed,
> We have brought home every load,
> Hip! Hip! Hip! Harvest home!

In September 1824, a lady traveller on the road to Bath came upon
an unaffected harvest vignette at Hawkesbury, in the high Cotswolds.
Under a maypole decorated with flowers and ribbons, stood a waggon loaded with men, women and children, corn and flowers, and
the horses were not forgotten for 'Scarlet bows and sunflowers had
been lavished on their winkers with no niggard hand. On the first
horse sat a damsel, no doubt intending to represent Ceres; she had on,
of course, a white dress and straw bonnet—for could Ceres, or any
other goddess appear in a rural English festival in any other costume?
A broad yellow sash encompassed a waist that evinced a glorious and
enormous contempt for classical proportion . . .'[22]

Day-long preparations went on for the great feast after harvest in
barn or kitchen, variously called harvest-home, mell-supper or feast-
of-ingathering, apart from Christmas, the most important meal of the
rural year and one of the rare occasions when beef brightened the
labourers' meagre diet. In northern England the churn-supper or
cream-pot came first when the corn was cut; near Bridlington in
1827 supper was of cream and currant- or seed-cakes marked with a
cross; and time passed pleasantly as the reapers danced round bonfires
in the field, ran races and blacked each others' faces with burned
straw, 'the lads aiming for the lasses, and the lasses for the lads'. Even
the dignified farmer's wife herself did not escape.[23]

As late as 1898 the mell-supper was part of North Riding life,
although its observance was beginning to fade. Farmer Robinson of
Carthorpe, among others, preserved the pleasant old ways and as in
Jutland the last sheaf was the 'widow', carried home in triumph
bound with ribbons (raced for by the women) and handkerchiefs (the
men's prize)—reminders of the day when the precious sheaf itself was
the trophy.

The harvest-cart at Hawkesbury, Gloucestershire

The day before the harvest feast of 1796 on her Herefordshire farm, Anne Hughes was busy with good things: six big chickens, three hares, beef and a bacon chine were cooking; two hams, a new cheese, tarts, custards, honey and gingercakes and plum-puddings; home-made wines, brandy, beer, cider and plenty of tobacco stood ready. Early next day the tables, decorated with ribbon-tied box sprays from the garden, were set in the best kitchen and the guests, and choir with fiddles ready for dancing, arrived at six o'clock. A merry evening followed and toasts and cheers flew back and forth until well after midnight.[24] At West Dorset harvest-homes, about 1870, the gates of the principal farms were decorated with arches of ever-greens, flowers and corn, crowned with a sickle and scythe, swathed in wheat and barley, with mottoes.

> Here's a health unto our master,
> The founder of the feast,
> God bless his endeavours and give him increase,
> God send him good crops that we may meet another year,
> Here's our master's good health boys, come drink off your beer!

soared to the rafters in Northamptonshire barns and this flexible song supported the remotest branches of the farmer's family, each new relationship an excuse for more ale. 'Now then, gentlemen, don't delay harmony' cried one hospitable Cotswold farmer-host, and they did not.[25] Farmer John Bussell of Whitchurch Canonicorum, Dorset, always concluded his harvest supper by performing the broomstick dance, a notable feat at that point of the evening.[26]

On a Wiltshire farm in 1911, a year of record harvest when many hill farms had cut, carried and threshed by 27 July, the affectionate toast at the evening's end was 'Hooray for the master, missis and our young miss'.[27] Feasts of the past were remembered, dramas of harvest, races against weather and, as much to the harvestmen of bygone years, as to the present lamplit circle of flushed faces, they sang the best-loved of all harvest songs:

> Here's a health to the barley-mow,
> Here's a health to the man,
> Who very well can
> Both harrow and plough and sow.

Page 33 The corn maiden, made by Mrs E. White of Northaw, Hertfordshire

Page 34 (above) Ploughing-match competitors near Berwick, Nova Scotia, 1971; (below) the cricket team at Rectory Farm, Waddesdon, about 1908 about to play a harvest-end match against a neighbouring farm. Mr T. G. Goss, the farmer, stands in the centre, straw hat in hand and another player holds a cider jar

When it is well sown,
See it is well mown,
Both raked and gavell'd clean,
And a barn to lay it in.
Here's a health to the man,
Who very well can
Both thrash and fan it clean.

Harvest rituals cast their glow into the twentieth century. Mr H. Wickett of Willey Farm, Sticklepath, often took part in a ceremony at Bradworthy in north-west Devon in which the last sheaf was bound and hoisted on to a pole in the harvest-field, to stand until the last waggon was loaded; its removal proclaimed the end of harvest and farmers competed keenly to be the first to lower it. The immemorial shout of 'Harvest-home!' went up in the rickyard, echoing for miles across the tranquil Devon plain, just as Hone's friend had heard it a century before. In the North Riding of Yorkshire harvest poetry survives; mell cakes are sent round on Westerdale farms and the last sheaf, ceremonially tied with twisted straw bands, is brought to the house with the exultant message 'We've getten t'mell' the first stage of harvest is over.[28] And only a few years ago an East Yorkshire farmer was seen to lay his last sheaf carefully aside to be spread on his newly-ploughed fields in spring, as his father and grandfather had done before him, an earnest of future harvests and a propitiation of the fickle corn-spirit.[29]

2

On the Farm:
Stock, Dairy and Orchard

Cattle were general providers, their importance confirmed daily in intimate routines of cowshed and dairy. Oxen, stronger than horses and cheaper to feed, played (and in Nova Scotia still play) a role as draught animals. In 1912 a Sussex auctioneer raised the good price of £46 for Frost and Fairman, £41 for Rock and Ruby and £37 each for Lark and Linnet, Turk and Tiger, although he remarked that these would probably be the last working oxen he would ever sell.[1]

One of each pair of oxen was given a single-syllabled and the other a two-syllabled name. There were other cattle-naming traditions: a correspondent in *Notes and Queries*, May 1850, remarked that in Somerset bulls were invariably called William. In 1906 teams were ploughing on Landport Farm, under the very walls of Lewes, Arthur Beckett was impressed by a team of black oxen from Chyngton Farm at a ploughing match near Beachy Head in 1909 and the last ox-team in Sussex worked at Birling Manor Farm, Eastdean as late as 1929.[2] A farmer who kept oxen was, by tradition, drawn to his burial by the team.

Despite their practical qualities cattle were vulnerable to witchcraft, but rowan sprigs plaited round their horns or nailed in cowstalls (still done on Exmoor) were effective deterrents. A witch might steal milk from distant cowsheds by hanging a plaited 'ladder' from her window and at proper milking times the cows gave little milk (a convenient explanation for a falling milk-yield). When a house at Wellington, Somerset, was demolished in 1887 a witch's-ladder, a

36

five-foot long rope stuck with cock's feathers, locally said to have assisted milk-stealing, was found in the attic.[3] Hallowed materials were useful in counter-measures. Wax from Easter candles was dropped on the cows' horns and left crosswise under the cowshed step and as late as 1850 in Ontario a wisewoman made the sign of the cross on bewitched beasts.[4] Even in 1920 young cattle from the Forest Ridge of Sussex were frequently seen at market with a tarred string or old bootlace threaded through a hole pierced in their dewlaps to save them from being 'struck' by the evil eye.

Magic governed the choice of droving-stick. Willow, said to injure cows, was unpopular, but benevolent hazel and rowan would fatten a beast and ash never caused injury. Holly brought back runaway cattle after whom it was thrown and a sprig in the cowshed made the cows thrive. Worcestershire farmers gave their Christmas mistletoe to the first cow to calve in the New Year, or put a little stolen hay in the Christmas Day feed, to bring luck to the dairy. A four-leafed clover hidden in the byre countered evil of all kinds, and cattle thrived in a field in which a magical hawthorn grew.

To be 'elf-shot' was a strange accident of the cowhouse: 'Bewitch'd, shot by fairies. Country people tell odd tales of this distemper amongst cows. When elf-shot the cow falls down suddenly dead; no part of the skin is pierced, but often a little triangular flat stone is found near the beast, as they report, which is called the elf's arrow.' It was a common affliction and a convenient explanation of cattle disorders which struck with few symptoms, as from a clear sky:

> ... ev'ry herd by sad experience knows
> How, wing'd with fate, their elf-shot arrows fly,
> When the sick ewe her summer food foregoes,
> Or stretch'd on earth the heart-smit heifers lie.[5]

The 'arrows', often found below ground near the dead beast, were in fact small fossil belemnites or flint slivers, quite unconnected with the animal's death; but the cure was thought to be water in which the 'arrows' had been dipped.

The naturally-holed flint, hag or limmell-stone, reminiscent of the all-seeing eye of ancient mythology, and a universal apotropaic or protective device, would nullify the glance of the 'evil-eye', was an indispensable amulet in cowshed, stable and house and may still be found in northern cow-byres, although no longer valued in the old way. It was a sure remedy against witchcraft, especially 'hag-riding', when fairies or witches took horses or cattle from their stalls, rode them hard all night and returned them sweating and weary, manes and tails inextricably tangled. Cautious farmers still tie their stable-keys to a hag-stone, pragmatically safeguarding the key but also creating a potent defensive charm from iron and holed stone. A holed flint in the village museum at Ashwell, Hertfordshire hung at a local farm for at least 150 years. Attempts made about 1930 to remove it for cleaning were strenuously resisted by the horsekeeper, but by 1952 the farm had given up horses and the flint was lent to the museum on the strict understanding that it be removed by a stranger and returned promptly should ill-effects follow.

The charm, calming to horses and cows (more often disturbed by digestive disorders, rats, tramps or smugglers, than by fairies), was known from one side of England to the other. When a Woodbridge butcher bought a calf from a farmer in June 1833, he remarked as he left the crib that 'the crater was all o' a muck, and desired the farmer to hang a flint by a string in the crib, just high enough to be clear of the calf's head; "Becaze," says he, "the calf is rid every night by the farisees and the stone will brush them off." '[6] About 1940–1 when collecting old agricultural implements in Swaledale, Mrs Olive Bedford found a hag-stone still hanging on a cowshed wall[7] and General Pitt Rivers took charge of a holed-stone which he noticed near Salisbury on the housedoor of a carter who believed it would keep witches away.[8]

Implements of safeguarding iron, especially those of cross-shape, were further deterrents to hag-riders:

> Hang up Hooks, and Sheers to scare
> Hence the Hag, that rides the Mare,
> Till they be all over wet,
> With the mire, and the sweat:
> This observ'd, the Manes shall be
> Of your horses, all knot-free.

Three valued remedies for cattle disease in the north of England were the Black Penny, owned by the Turnbull family, Northumberland; the silver Lockerby Penny from Dumfriesshire—after one farmer's death, bottles carefully labelled 'Lockerby Water' were found among his effects—and most famous, the Lee Penny, a dark red stone set in a silver coin of Edward I and belonging to a Scottish family. All were dipped in water which the sick beasts drank, and until well into the nineteenth century farmers travelled far to borrow them. It was widely believed that only a silver bullet would kill an animal such as a hare or fox whose mantle a witch had assumed for nefarious purposes. Silver in cowshed or dairy was equally effective against witchcraft and an 'eye-smitten' person, too, was given 'silver-water' to drink.

Up to the mid-nineteenth century, barbaric remedies of a propitiatory nature were sometimes found in use on farms. Veterinary science was slow to take hold in remoter areas and small farmers often could not afford professional advice, even if they had wished it. In 1853 a Devon farmer at Meavy, some of whose stock had died, burned a sacrificial sheep on Catesham Tor. No more cattle died and the well-satisfied farmer was happy to tell his vicar, the Rev W. A. G. Gray, of his action, as though it were nothing extraordinary, as it probably was not. The charmer even now has his place in the cowshed. Mrs R. E. St Leger-Gordon writes in *The Witchcraft and Folklore of Dartmoor* of a young couple who within recent years completed training at an agricultural college and settled down to farm in Devon. Almost at once their dairy herd was attacked by ringworm. To their surprise the Ministry of Agriculture veterinary surgeon to whom they turned referred them to a local charmer or white witch who lived nearby, saying 'He'll charm your cows for you.' Somewhat hesitantly they followed this suggestion and the treatment was completely successful.[9] Within living memory East Anglian farmers buried a *slinked* or aborted calf under the cowshed doorstep to break a sequence of sickness, and part of a dead cow might be quietly left on a neighbour's farm to transfer disease. During an outbreak of foot-and-mouth disease in Britain in 1967–8 a Cheshire farmer's wife attributed her farm's escape (although ringed by infection) to onions—important in folk-medicine—which she set about the cowsheds. Within the last century ailing Sussex cattle were driven under an arched bramble spray, symbolising healthy rebirth, and Shropshire cows were fed biblical texts with their hay. Good Friday bread in cider made a curative mash. In a more formal rite during the cattle plague of 1747, a dirge of eight stanzas sung in Osmotherley church, Yorkshire described the deceased cattle, naming their owners, and continued:

> No Christian's bull nor cow, they say,
> But takes it out of hand;
> And we shall have no cows at all,
> I doubt, within this land . . .
>
> So Heaven drive out this plague away,
> And vex us not no more.[10]

Hedgehogs and adders in England, believed to suck cows at pasture, and in Ontario the eastern hognosed snake, of alarming appearance but harmless habits, whose breath farmers said, would cause a cow's death are still sometimes killed on sight. Throughout North America the milk snake is said to steal milk from dairy pans and cows, although it merely visits farm buildings and water-troughs during hot weather when the milk-yield drops naturally, circumstances now linked in agricultural lore.

Calving is a superstition-ridden process; the farmer must guard against putting his hand on the calf's back or it will suffer 'scour', nor must he set his stable-lantern down upon a table or the cow may slip her calf prematurely—beliefs alive today. Farmers ('only stopped by the milk inspectors') carefully hung the afterbirth upon the hawthorn —noted for quick growth and health and sometimes called quickset in exposition of these excellent qualities—a tree as trouble-free as any farmer could wish his herd to be. By sympathetic magic the future fertility of the herd and its freedom from milk-fever was thus assured. About 1850 a farmer at Edgmond, Shropshire, caught his old servant thrusting hair into a cow's ear. The man explained that it was specially cut from the calf's tail by the butcher who collected the animal, and that the act would make her forget her calf. Similarly, in the United States, if a cow ate some of her own hair after a change of farm, she would forget her old home.

The pre-eminence of the horse in battle and ancient religions, his links with harvest and the corn-spirit and his importance until recent years as the major agricultural motive-power, made horse-magic, known to blacksmiths and horsekeepers, the most potent on the farm. Indeed it is still remembered by the oldest generation of countrymen. Many an unexpected visitor to harness-room, forge or stable, noticed a silence fall among the men as they swiftly drew together and thrust secret mixtures into cornbins or dark corners away from the stranger's curious gaze. In his presidential address to the anthropology section of the British Association in 1971, George Ewart Evans said that he had found traces of the old magic in East Anglia, an arable area where the horse was formerly of the greatest importance. There, horsemen often belonged to small secret societies devoted to horse-magic or at least shared the same ritualistic practices. Their awesome initiation required them to go to running water at midnight, at full moon, to perform a rite with a frog or toad bone which, ground to powder and mixed with 'dragon's blood' (a code name for a substance attractive to horses, unconnected with the resin of the *Dracaena draco* tree), would give a man complete control over a horse. A little of this in a hand laid on a horse's shoulder, an old Suffolk horseman named Charlie told Mr Evans, would cause the horse to kneel as though saying his prayers.[11] The bones and the ritual, although part of the cult, apparently played no intrinsic role, except as carriers for 'drawing' and 'jading' substances. The latter, with elements offensive to the horse's delicate sense of smell, stopped an animal so that it would not move against the charmer's wishes; the bone was dipped into or cured with strong-smelling herbs and chemicals before it went into the horseman's pocket ready for use, to be placed in front of the horse to halt him, or behind to urge him forward to escape it. Attractive to the horse were 'drawing' or 'calling' oils. A farmer advised Molly Hankey whose unruly young pony was running on Bodmin Moor, to put a mixture of fifteen drops of aniseed, ten drops each of oils of cinnamon and nutmeg, rosemary, thyme, tincture of opium, and two drachms of lunia or orris-root powder, on the pony's nose, to induce, he said, complete obedience. Mrs Hankey had no opportunity of testing the receipt, but it was undoubtedly one of the old drawing potions.[12]

These substances and practices, and the whispered charm of the 'horseman's word', which bound horsemen to their society, were so well-guarded that there is now little definite knowledge of forms, although hints are found in notebooks of old horsekeepers and in the oral tradition. Through them vicious animals became docile, the hard-to-catch came to hand, runaways were instantly halted, the restless became easy to shoe and horses followed charmers (who gained considerable prestige from their 'gift') for miles. Or of course the potions could be used malevolently to make the docile intractable, and to score off other horsemen. Such practices (and the enduring aversion to horseflesh as food is another), are reminders of the horse's role in primitive cultures, of which remnants lingered in half perceived form until recent years, particularly in the relative isolation of eastern England.

Arthur Randell had first-hand experience of horsecharmers' powers when, near Wisbech, one Sunday morning in 1927, he arranged with a local farmer, Mr H. Flint of Friday Bridge, to borrow two horses to move a railway wagon destined to become a pigsty. The head horse-keeper was out on his paper round, but the second horseman, Pal Day, agreed to bring the horses to the station yard where they were hitched to the wagon and moved it without difficulty. The party paused to discuss rounding a corner and at that moment the head horsekeeper passed and bet Mr Randell and Mr Day that the wagon would move no further that day. And strain as they might, the horses could not move it an inch further. The farmer was astonished at this news but enquired if the head horseman's approval had been sought before the horses were borrowed, suggesting that he be approached before another attempt was made. This was done (with a small financial encouragement) and at the next attempt one mare alone moved the wagon with ease. The farmer explained that the head man could bewitch horses so effectively that they would not move against his wishes; he was vexed at not being consulted at the outset and had taken his revenge. Forty-five years later, in 1972, Mr Randell told the writer: 'I still have the old railway wagon that the horses couldn't move that first Sunday; it's surprising how many people have visited me just to see the old truck and to hear me tell the tale all over again . . .'[13]

Collars of holly and bittersweet saved horses from witchcraft, and whips with holly-wood handles were favoured by Fenland coachmen after dark; but the tree was magical and no branch must be *cut* for whipstock-making; it was safer to pull up the long shoots about the trunk. 'If your whipstick's made of rowan, you may ride your horse through any town', and an elder twig in a rider's pocket is a valuable charm against saddle-soreness.

Some amulets bore the imaginative imprint of their inventors; a Norfolk horseman seen driving his horse around 1850 had placed on a cord about its neck the thumb of an old glove containing a transcript of the Lord's Prayer, against all ills, he said, including stumbling. Horse-brasses, whose shapes include wheel, sun and crescent, are generally thought protective amulets, although significantly there seems little knowledge of this in the great horse-keeping areas of East Anglia where brasses were purely decorative. A part of every working horse's equipment, and the property of the carter, brasses went with him from job to job to set off prized teams. Decorative, protective against witchcraft and practical, were tinkling cup, crotal or rumbler bells suspended in groups of two, three or four between the hames. An elderly Sussex woman told Viscountess Wolseley about 1920 that she could distinguish the bells on her husband's team when he was still four miles from home.[14]

Brilliant worsted braids or hounces worn on the collars if the team left farm for highroad and still seen on brewers' horses, are both ornamental and protective in origin, for a witch, particularly deterred by red braid (red thread and rowan form a potent amulet against the evil eye), must count the threads before harming the team. As a further deterrent, waggons were painted in strong colours, scarlet, blue or yellow, a practice carried forward in the bright paint of agricultural machinery on both sides of the Atlantic. In the last century 'Scotch' carts appeared in East Anglia, traditionally decorated with a pair of eyes, sometimes elaborated as 'spectacles' or 'butterfly wings', forward-facing to deflect an evil eye directed at cart or horse.[15]

Horses were rested on Old Christmas Day lest they be difficult all the year, and Good Friday and New Year's Day were similar holidays for beasts. Many blacksmiths flatly refused to shoe on Good Friday, even in emergencies, part of a general reluctance to use iron in any form then. A colt's first shoeing, frequently a lively occasion, was often marked by a little ceremony—in East Anglia 'the first nail'—when a shilling was added to the farmer's bill for celebratory beer in the forge afterwards.

Gleaming teams of horses spoke of the farm's prosperity ('If poverty gets into the stable, it is soon all over the house'). Hundreds of semi-magical and herbal remedies formed the horsekeeper's armoury against disease and are perhaps still administered from time to time. Bleeding of horses and oxen, general on St Stephen's Day as late as the eighteenth century, was thought beneficial to all draught animals. One Dorset ploughman, whose horses' condition was admired, dropped worms into an old tin on his plough-handles, corking them up to form a clear oil which he mixed with his team's feed.[16] Savin, *Juniperus sabina*, was a conditioner, abortifacient and contraceptive, used by cunning old horsemen who did not wish their mares to benefit from the stallion's visit. For those who *did*, bryony (for mandrake) was a fertility stimulant. Elecampane—horseheal—an appetite improver with bitter aromatic leaves was another plant likely to be cultivated by horsekeepers. Mouse-ear hawkweed, *Herba clavorum*, the herb of nails, protected horses from shoeing injuries, but moonwort, a close-growing fern, had the reputation of removing the shoes of any horse which stepped upon it: thirty horses of the Earl of Essex suffered thus on White Down, Tiverton, Devon.[17]

Mares were mated at the moon's increase for healthy, quick-growing foals and Suffolk farmers ensured that the sun never shone in a stallion's eyes when he served a mare—lest, by sympathetic magic, the progeny have generally disliked white feet. Like May cats and sows, May-born horses were considered unreliable and all horses tended to be troublesome in this witching month but a horse born on Midsummer Day was favoured and would become master horse of any team.

SHEEP AND PIGS

Honeycomb smocking on shepherds' smocks or round-frocks traditionally varied in design from county to county and a shepherd's origins were assessed at a sheep-fair by his smock. In some counties, shepherds were buried in their tough, weather-proof linen smocks, an extension of the widespread practice of laying a lock of sheepswool in a shepherd's coffin, for at judgement day deficiencies in his church attendance would thus be attributed to a demanding calling. Smocks, the countryman's working dress (paralleled on the American frontier by the practical hunting-shirt), were in general farm use within living memory, particularly in Sussex, although they had died out by about 1914. The Rev A. J. Roberts, vicar of Harting, remembered that about 1889 he would see as many as fifty best smocks in his Whitsun congregation, but by 1909 only one or two.

Sheep-shearing, usually in June (and if possible at the moon's increase to enhance the wool's bulk), was the pleasantest event in the farmer's year; work combined with play awaited neighbours who lent a hand for no other reward than hearty meals and a sociable summer outing:

> Wife, make us a dinner, spare fleshe neither corn,
> Make wafers and cakes for our sheepe must be shorne;
> At sheep-shearing, neighbours none other things crave,
> But good cheere and welcome like neighbours to have.

wrote Thomas Tusser of Elizabethan England but things were little changed in nineteenth-century Devon, writes Miss Trump; 'At sheep-shearing parties the young men of the farms would go from one farm to another to shear the sheep. Hard-working days those, but the young men were tough, for later the ladies would arrive and sheep-shearing days were followed by dancing evenings and youngsters would shear all day and dance half the night.' Retired shepherds walked miles to 'have a look' at the day's proceedings and in Vermont also, once wool capital of the United States, the visitors enjoyed the best the farm could offer.

In a vein of pastoral poetry Sussex shearing parties sang:

> Here the rosebuds in June and the violets are blooming,
> The small birds they warble from every green bough;
> Here's the pink and the lily,
> And the daffadowndilly,
> To adorn and perfume the sweet meadows in June.
> 'Tis all before the plough the fat oxen go slow,
> But the lads and the lasses to the sheep-shearing go.

Shearers elected a captain and lieutenant in gold and silver-laced hats[18] and in Devon changed into white duck 'shearing suits' (which would be filthy at the end of the day) before starting work. At dinner-time the men washed their hands in pails of water in which sprigs of wild flowering mint floated, for nothing removed grease and smell so effectively. Later 'drinkings' were brought out to the barn by the girls—' "cut-rounds" already spread with cream, or gingerbread, and mugs of tea, and the men were nothing loath to straighten their backs and stretch their legs, for three minutes, before they cried once more, "Sheep ho!" ' remembered Hannah Cox O'Neill in *Devonshire Idyls*, 1892, of Buzacott Farm, Devon, fifty years before. Work ceased at 8 and by 9 all were washed and ready for supper. Farmer Butter sat at the top of the table in the old hall to carve a big round of boiled beef and several squab pies, Aunt Charity handed round plates of junket and cream when the meat was removed, and 'a big jug of strong shearing ale, brewed last Fall, and half a new cheese was set before the master. Tall old-fashioned glasses, each with a barley-ear and a droop of hops engraved at the rim were served round, and each man filled for himself as the big jug made its circuit.'[19]

The feats of the shearers astonished all who saw them. 'John Pinkney of Aiskew,' wrote Mr Naitby, a Bedale schoolmaster, in 1845, 'did accomplish a wonderful piece of shearing in that of his own hand he did draw from the pen 150 sheep and shear the same, and bind his own fleeces and within the space of 36 hours, or three full days' work. I hold there be few to match against him.'[20] Northamptonshire girls gave their sweethearts 'clipping-posies' of cabbage roses, pansies, pea flowers, monkshood, gillyflowers, wallflowers, columbines, gorse, snapdragons, pinks and lavender, all bound with marjoram, sweetbriar and ribbon grass.[21]

Shepherds still return strays to their flocks at friendly North Country sheep-meets. Junketings once lasted from Friday to Wednesday at the famous Mardale meet while the sheep waited patiently in their pens under clear autumn skies and the shepherds in the inn enjoyed the traditional 'tatie pot'—mutton and potatoes—with pickles, apple pie and cheese, and such songs as 'Joe Bowman' (the legendary Lakeland huntsman) and 'The Mardale Hunt', roared out to blasts from the hunting horn.

Within living memory the flat chime of sheepbells on the downland breeze was part of life in Wiltshire, Sussex and other sheep counties, protecting the flock from both witchcraft and straying. Shepherds owned their bells—40 was a usual number—worn by the most venturesome ewes and bells were inherited, not bought, the farmer paying only for replacements and repairs. A few Wiltshire farmers still use bells for their pleasant associations.[22]

Witchcraft was an ever-present threat. In 1846 a Yorkshire writer scornfully observed lambs with rowan collars playing in the fields, and in 1957 an informant recalled that the shepherd at Crowcombe Court, Somerset, stuck a dead sheep's heart with pins to exorcise evil spirits assailing his charges. Twigs from a shrew-ash, in which a live shrew was immured, an infallible cure for ills, especially palsy, caused, shepherds claimed, by shrews running over a sheep's back, awaited emergencies. A vicar near Yarm, Yorkshire, noticing hazel catkins stuck round the kitchen fireplace one spring day was told that his young servant, Jane, believed that this was 'good for sheep at lambing time'. In this homely charm, catkins, analogous to lambs' tails (and so called by country children), were linked with the hearth, powerful in magic. Lambs were never castrated or docked of tails at the moon's wane, or they would lose condition. Church ivy, saved from Christmas decorations and fed to ewes, induced the conception of twin lambs.

May-farrowing sows were carefully watched for they might eat their litters in accord with the month's sinister reputation. In Cheshire, until at least 1934, sows were invariably given rounds of bread and butter for luck as soon as their piglets were born, and when margarine was suggested instead, the idea was poorly received.[23] Rowan garlands, securing quick fattening, countered pig-bewitchment and in Nova Scotia hung in ailing pigs' sties.

Many were the stories of enchantment. Mr G. Fowles of East Stour, Dorset, who died during the 1920s, worked as a boy for a farmer near Wells, Somerset, whose pigs were pronounced bewitched. A wiseman advised the burning of hairs from the pigs' backs at midnight. As the hairs touched the flames the anxious operators in the kitchen were startled by a great bang on the housedoor and in terror fled to their beds, but from that moment the pigs enjoyed perfect health. D. St Leger-Gordon wrote of an old Devonshire woman in the Torridge valley with the 'evil eye'. Visiting, she and her daughter passed some small pigs in the rectory farmyard and she exclaimed 'Oh, the pretty dear!' pointing at a particular piglet, which fell dead in full view of the astonished clergyman. Her daughter, shocked at such irreverence, cried, 'I never thought you'd ha' done it, mother, to *Parson's* pig!'[24] Even in 1924 a summons was served on a farmer at Clyst St Lawrence, Devon, for assaulting an old woman he accused of bewitching his pigs.[25]

Bawdy competitions, felicitously called 'Venus nights', were held in the village inns of Cambridgeshire for the most strikingly anthropomorphic bryony root (for mandrake) in female form. The prize-winning root, powerful in sympathetic magic, hung in the sow's sty to induce large litters, and when withered was dropped into the household money-stocking as a stimulant there. Bryony also served as a general pig tonic and Arthur Randell always kept a root or two in his pig-troughs.

THE ORCHARD

In the West of England until the last century (and the practice continues, without magical intention), it was the custom to 'wassail' apple trees in a fertility ritual encouraging good crops in the coming year. 'In the South-Hams of Devonshire on the Eve of the Epiphany, the farmer attended by his workmen goes to the orchard with a large pitcher of cyder, and there, encircling one of the best bearing trees, they drink the following toast three times:

> Here's to thee, old apple-tree,
> Whence thou may'st bud, and whence thou may'st blow!
> And whence thou may'st bear apples enow!
> Hatsfull! Capsfull!
> Bushel-bushel-sacksfull,
> And my pockets full too! Huzza!

Some are so superstitious as to believe that if they neglect this custom the trees will bear no apples that year,' noted *The Gentleman's Magazine* in 1791.

The party dipped clomes or earthenware cups into the cider, threw some into the branches, left cider-soaked toast 'for the robin' (or orchard-god), and beat a loud tattoo on pots and pans to wake the sleeping tree-spirits. The farmer fired his gun, shots echoing through the frost-dark branches of the winter trees, and the company bowed three times, raising themselves encouragingly, as if carrying heavy sacks. Wassaillers still visit the orchard at the Butcher's Arms, Carhampton on Old Twelfth Night, and farmers fire their guns under the snow-clouds, but as Laurence Whistler points out, the orchard laughter has grown lighthearted with the years.[26] It was not always so. Wassailling is also observed in the great apple-growing region round Yakima, Washington, introduced by some who had visited Carhampton.

The kindly West Country custom of 'griggling' continues in Somerset, where children are allowed (and were once encouraged, since the farmer's wife had bread, cheese, cider and pennies for them) to steal the little apples ('the piskies harvest'), left on the trees. Mrs D. D. Houlton of Burford, Oxfordshire, wrote in 1972, when 81, that Cotswold children asked mother for permission to go 'a-scraggling' provided they did not 'dub'—throw sticks to knock fruit down.[27] At Newington, Kent, the cherry crop is blessed when the blossom is at its finest and until recently 'blessing the blossoms' took place annually in the cherry orchards at Traverse City, Michigan.[28] Less formally, rain on St Swithin's Day blesses the crop of waxen green July apples. On 15 July 1870 a Huntingdonshire cottager said, pointing to his apple trees: 'I shall get a few o' them codlins for a dumplin' for my Sabbath dinner. I never taste an apple till the Sabbath after St Swithin', and quoted the old saying:

> Till St Swithin's Day be past
> The apples be not fit to taste.[29]

Flowers and fruit together on the tree (a not unusual occurrence) are an ominous sign from Somerset to Maryland, portending a family death. In Yorkshire a small apple is left as a propitiatory gift and care is taken to thank the tree for its fruit. Within living memory in Devon, 'hoard' or keeping apples were picked in the moon's dark, lest her harmful rays cause rot, but grafts were successful and fruit trees grew straighter if pruning and grafting were done at the increase. Tusser advised:

> From moon being changed,
> Till past be the prime,
> For graffing [sic] and cropping,
> Is very good time.

Sympathetic magic requires that the work be done by a young and healthy man, a belief extant in Maryland. And holed stones strung on wire, seen between two ancient apple trees at Frogham, Hampshire, in the 1950s, suggest that this valuable amulet plays its part in protecting orchard as much as house and cowshed.[30]

THE DAIRY

The dairy, affected by temperature, bacterial deficiencies or dairymaids' carelessness, was a natural home for witchcraft; 'Should the "auld witch" call ... during the operation of churning, and be suffered to depart without a sop being thrown to her, in the shape of a small print of butter, you will be sure to have many a weary hour of labour the next time you churn ... to prevent the old beldam introducing herself into the churn, the churn-staff must be of the "*Wiggen* Tree", and you will be effectually freed from her further interference,' a Westmorland correspondent told Hone about 1826.[31]

Yorkshire dairymaids kept a crooked silver sixpence on the house witchpost for a 'churn-spell' should the butter not come, John Hughes dropped a crown piece into the cream for this purpose on 6 February 1796, 'drop a dime into it' was Kentucky advice, reduced to a five-cent piece in Nova Scotia, and a redhot poker or horseshoe thrust into the cream (actually producing the 60°F required for buttermaking), 'killed the witch'. Ashwood, feared by witches, was chosen for milk-pails and safeguarding hazel sticks for stirring milk in cooling troughs, to keep fairies away.

A long-lived butter-charm, seriously employed in Berkshire even in 1900, dates from at least 1553–8. A seventeenth-century account of its use tells how an old woman came to the house after a fruitless

Page 51 (above) Horses wearing crotal bells delivering hop pockets from Trimmers Farm at Alton station, Hampshire in 1899. From the Hampshire County Museum Service collection; (below) the fourteenth-century tithe barn at Lacock, Wiltshire, the property of the National Trust

Page 52 A bar-raising at North Danville, Vermont, about 1880–90. The frame is complete, the men have climbed to the topmost beams and the elders and women, who have prepared the feast that will follow, stand below. From the Vermont Historical Society's Photographic Archives

buttermaking session and 'told the maid what was wont to be done when she was a maid, and also in her mother's young time, that if it happened then butter would not come readily, they used a charm to be said over it . . .

> Come, butter, come,
> Come, butter, come,
> Peter stands at the gate
> Waiting for a butter'd cake;
> *Come*, butter, come.

This, said the old woman, being *said three times*, will make your butter come, for it was taught my mother by a learned churchman in Queen Marie's days, when as churchmen had more cunning and could teach the people many a trick that our ministers now a days know not.'[32]

A Yorkshire girl marrying a farmer would receive from her mother a wedding-present of a 'butter-penny'—a heavy, new penny—to lie upon the butterscale with the 'pundstan', a natural one-pound stone weight, so that no customer at the farm dairy could complain of short measure.[33]

John Aubrey reminded cheesemakers of the luck-giving significance of the number seven, in the dairy as elsewhere:

> If you will have a good cheese and hav'n old,
> You must turn'n seven times before he's cold.[34]

And this precept was followed by many generations of dairymaids to ensure exact blending of curd. Pastures were 'broken' or opened to cattle on Old May Day, significantly the first day of Celtic summer and cheesemaking then began. At Hornsea and Southorp in the East Riding of Yorkshire, before the enclosures, the milkmaids collected flowers to be made into garlands at the house of the nowtherd, or cowherd, on Whit-Sunday and there enjoyed cold posset and 'white cakes'. On the Monday morning the first milkmaid to reach each pasture received a ribbon and was named 'queen' or 'lady' of that pasture for the summer, girls anxious to gain this coveted honour sat up all night to make their entrances at 3am. A dinner at the nowtherd's followed, with dancing until milking-time, and gaiety went on for several days in a specially decorated barn.[35] During late summer butter was salted and potted for winter use but work stopped when the ash-leaves fell:

> Farmers' wives, when the leaves do fall
> 'Twill spoil your milk and butter and all

While some said, prosaically, that leaves eaten by cows made the milk bitter, the magical reputation of the ash, an influential tree in the dairy, may well have entered into it.

BARNS AND RICKS

Walter Rose called the clean and fragrant barn the parlour of the farm. Here the rhythmic thump-thump of flails on old threshing-floors high polished by constant use was heard after harvest, and picked up in one barn after another through the village as the back-breaking work went forward. The flail handle was usually of ash and the 'swingle', the shorter piece of the 'stick-and-a-half', of holly or hawthorn, all protective woods, although selected in this instance, their users maintained, for hard-wearing qualities. Flailing is not quite forgotten; in 1947 at Ley Farm, Luccombe, Exmoor, corn was still being threshed thus against a chained barrel in the farmyard.[36]

Engaging charms protected stored corn from rats; sometimes a hot cross bun kept from Good Friday hung in the granary as a deterrent charm, or crushed roots of mandrake or bryony were thrust down ratholes. Theo Brown notes that charming was successfully used at Broadclyst in 1963 to dispose of unwanted shrews and that mice had also been encouraged to leave in this way, by polite invitation. On 31 October 1888, the owner of a house in Maine wrote a friendly letter to his rats explaining that house alterations would make the coming winter uncomfortable and suggesting a move to a neighbouring farm, 'where you will find a splendid cellar well filled with vegetations of all kinds besides a shed leading to a barn with a good supply of grain where you can live snug and happy.' He concluded firmly, 'Shall do you no harm if you heed my advice, but if not shall employ "Rough on Rats".' This message, on well-greased paper, was poked into a rathole and even if not completely effective, drastically reduced the number of rats. In the mid-nineteenth century a Cheshire man at

'Griggling' in the orchard

Pruning apple trees, best done at the moon's increase

Peover could charm rats from one farm to another provided they did not have to cross a road. His employer, who had annoyed him, was warned he would regret it and soon afterwards found his farm 'snying' with rats. Later a potato clamp collapsed under their tunnelling.[37] And a Cornish farmer's wife near Truro was seen to lay a chain, not touching the ground, round her duckhouse to keep rats away, in another protective charm.[38]

Beams for a new house or barn were cut, numbered and taken to the building site to be hoisted into position, often by the whole male workforce of the village. Raising-parties were known in Yorkshire as late as 1898; at thatching-time a bottle was suspended from the ridge beam and whoever threw the stone which broke the bottle claimed the ribbon which held it. After the English pattern, buildings were cheerfully christened in pioneer North America, with, on one occasion at least, an important difference. 'Once at a raising near Ancaster,' wrote Benjamin Waldbrook of Oakville, Ontario, in the early nineteenth century, 'I saw a man, bottle in hand, run up the peak where the two rafters joined. There, balancing on one foot he sang out:

> It is a good framing,
> And shall get a good naming,
> And what shall the naming be?

When the prearranged name was shouted, the man on the rafters so declared it, as he cast the bottle to the ground. Was the bottle broken? No indeed! As it contained the best liquor supplied at the raising, care was taken to see that it fell on soft ground.'[39]

Ricks are still sometimes finished with green branch or straw cock-bird finial, which gleams across a full rickyard, once preventing witches from landing on the rickridge, and keeping fire, lightning and tempest at bay. Making rick ornaments is a living craft. 'The farmer who has our land is not only an artist at thatching or 'theeacking ricks,' writes Major Fairfax-Blakeborough from Westerdale, 'but also at making decorations for each.' Common rick ornaments are crosses, crowns, birds and animals, not plaited as the corn dolly is, but made from folded bundles of straw tied with binder twine.[40]

3

House and Garden Magic

Superstition forms little part of household life today, but once, when disease, fire and other disasters were constant threats to domestic security, every means of protecting the house and its surroundings, the core of family life, was sought. Rituals and charms, carefully executed, confirmed a man's identity with his home, and formed the very framework for living. Although these procedures could clearly have no intrinsic influence on events, they were undeniably important to the occupants of the house; an affirmation that by confidently aligning their most intense desires with ritual acts, they might hope to remain masters of the situation and to bend fickle fortune in their favour.

PROTECTING THE HOUSE

Many amulets other than the ubiquitous horseshoe protected the house from malevolent forces. Mrs Margaret Gatty, wife of the vicar of Ecclesfield, Yorkshire, visiting a cottage at Catterick about 1850 noticed a 'ponderous necklace' of holed stones hanging behind the door. The old lady of the house, at first inclined to shuffle off an explanation, admitted finally that it was to keep the house from the evil eye. 'Why, Nanny,' said Mrs Gatty, 'you surely don't believe in witches now-a-days?' 'No! I don't say 'at I do; but certainly i' former times there *was* wizzards an' buzzards, and them sort o' things.' 'But surely you don't think there are any now?' 'No! I don't say 'at ther' are; but I *do* believe in a *yevil* eye', and it turned out that there was an old woman of the neighbourhood against whose malignity all believed it best to take precautions. Holed stones are still in use: two sets were found hanging on nails in a New Forest cottage about 1958.[1]

Cruciform 'Christian doors' of Nova Scotia, Maine and Cape Cod were another protective device[2] and cruciate or S-shaped braces attached to old housewalls lent metaphysical as well as structural strength with safeguarding iron. In a related practice builders in West Surrey and Buckinghamshire pressed small pieces of ironstone into wall pointings, originally to save houses from witchcraft. Gilbert White wrote of the usage (called 'garneting'): 'Strangers sometimes . . . ask us pleasantly "whether we fastened our walls together with tenpenny nails" ', for the pieces of stone were about the size of a three-inch nailhead. Gertrude Jekyll mentions the device, in *Old West Surrey*, 1904, and used it in her garden designs.[3] Reverence for iron began at the moment when its magical superiority over bronze and stone for weapons and implements was first appreciated and belief in its protective qualities is still evident in many superstitions. 'Cold iron' was truly a formidable substance to witch or enemy alike and the metal gathered heightened mysticism through its later use at the crucifixion.

Edward Peacock of Bottesford Manor, Brigg, Lincolnshire, reported in *Notes and Queries*, August 1867, that he had recently made alterations to the part of his house which had been a kitchen since 1757. About sixteen inches below ground was found a pavement, perhaps medieval, and some of its stones had been carefully lifted and pieces of old iron—forkheads, broken scythes and chains—neatly arranged in their place to halt a witch attempting entrance. In Cornwall a protective hot cross bun hung from the kitchen bacon-rack. Rowan witchposts, carved with billets and St Andrew's crosses, standing between chimney and door, supporting larger beams and smokehood, would prevent the entry of witches and are common in cottages in Eskdale, Yorkshire.[4] White-painted window-frames and whitewashed premises in general in Cornwall, and round Bridlington, Yorkshire, a thick white curtain within the window, were other safeguards.

Coloured glass 'witchballs' deflected an evil-intentioned glance, glass rolling-pins (filled with protective salt), and charmwands, favourite decorations for cottage walls, delayed a witch while she counted the decorative 'seeds' and spirals before turning her attention to the family. The wands—of which Strangers' Hall Museum, Norwich has a group—also attracted and held diseases harmlessly until the next day's dusting. Bottles stuffed with threads, red predominating, are still occasionally found in old houses during repair work, strategically placed up chimneys, under hearths or above doors, all places where the crone might seek entrance. And a bullock's heart stuck with new pins, point outwards, suspended in the chimney as a prophylactic charm would scratch her as she descended and no witch risked having blood drawn (and power nullified) thus. *The Bridport News* reported that in a cottage at Shipton, in April 1901, a chimney sweep had found a heart stuck with pins and thorns (the fourth to be found in the neighbourhood about that time), in a canvas bag hanging about ten feet up a chimney. And the same objects could be used with maleficent, not protective, intent; a victim's initials pricked upon a heart hung in the witch's chimney to scorch and smoke would cause the bewitched one great suffering.

The witch reached her victim by manipulating his hair cuttings, nail parings or urine, and these materials were useful in counter-attacks. The heating of a bottle of the sufferer's urine, with pubic hair, pins and broken glass, would cause the tormentor such sympathetic pain as to bring her to the house to reveal herself and perhaps trade spell for counter-spell; Herrick wrote explicitly of a like charm's method:

> To House the Hag, you must doe this;
> Commix with Meale a little Pisse
> Of him bewitcht: then forthwith make
> A little Wafer or a Cake;
> And this rawly bak't will bring
> The old Hag in. No surer thing.

About forty years ago a bottle, its cork studded with pins, apparently a countercharm, was found hanging by a wire in a farmhouse chimney at Winterbourne Kingston, Dorset. It contained liquid, perhaps urine, and when the bottle was accidentally broken the household's luck changed dramatically for the worse.[5] In a similar association of ideas, if milk boiled over on the fire, the housewife quickly sprinkled salt on the hissing cinders lest the udder of the cow which had given the milk become inflamed. Sometimes a 'Bellamine' salt-glazed jar, with decora-. tive bearded face, was used to parry spells; it was often buried (possibly with hair and nails, as a seventeenth-century example in the Castle Museum, Norwich, demonstrates) about house or field, or under hedgerow. As it disappeared from sight in the earth a specific spell was extinguished, or more broadly, stock, fields and house were safeguarded from a malevolent wish. The many finds of Bellamines included one found in the River Sherway at Smarden, Kent, in the winter of 1971–2, perhaps tossed into the stream to carry the spell towards the witch's or victim's house.

Such bottles showed the same two-fold role as chimney hearts and could be used as readily for evil as for protective purposes. A man digging in his garden at Yaddlethorpe, Lincolnshire about 1850, found a horse or ox skeleton about three feet below the surface and two bottles (one had held wine and the other Daffy's elixir) filled with pins, needles, human hair and a foetid fluid. Local people told him guardedly that was 'summut to do with witching'. And on 3 October 1872, when an earthen bank was levelled on Penrhos Bradwn Farm, Anglesey, a black pipkin was found, a slate covering its mouth. Scratched in rude letters on either side of the slate were the words 'Nanney Roberts' and inside was a dried frog pierced with 40 pins, clearly a relic of a malevolent charm.[6]

A house was believed to stand more fortunately for a sacrifice. In ancient times this was human, but later a man's shadow, or a dead animal, was felt to answer as well and by the later Middle Ages animal or bird bones were commonly used—and indeed are still often found by builders during restoration work, especially in eastern England. Horse-bones were discovered recently in the walls of a sixteenth-century cottage at Histon, Cambridgeshire; until recent years The Mitre at Oxford showed the skeleton of a small snake revealed during repairs, and at Gazeley, Suffolk, an ox's shinbone was traditionally incorporated into the thatch. Blood mixed with mortar made protective charms for hearth, chimney and house and the crumbling besom broom found within the wall of Dale House,

Blandford, in 1930, probably had like purpose. The owners prudently replaced it.

Shoes and other footwear, dating from the fifteenth to the twentieth centuries, are found built into house walls, over lintels, in chimneys and similar places, singly or very rarely in pairs, in 'families' or with such homely articles as purses, knives or mousetraps. Their purpose is not yet clear, but they may well have been apotropaic devices, connected with the strong human liking for well-used possessions preserved for arcane reasons of personal identity. Most of the shoes found are well worn, patched and occasionally slashed in a cross pattern. A recent cottage find at Eydon, Northamptonshire, included wine bottles, a woman's boot, two school exercise books, a slate, candle snuffers, a spoon and a clock key, all of about 1847 and worn and broken.

North American examples include a woman's and boy's boots of about 1850–60, with soles missing, found recently in the rafters of a house in Abbs Valley, Virginia, and a child's boot of apparently mid-nineteenth century date found during the 1940s near St David's, Ontario, in the kitchen wall of a house predating the War of 1812 and one of the few houses in St David's to escape burning by American troops then.[7]

'Blackthorn?' *Never* in my house,' said a Buckinghamshire blacksmith's wife in 1972. There is a widespread prejudice against blossom (whether blackthorn, apple, plum or pear) indoors. Hawthorn has an ambivalent reputation; the twigs are protective if gathered on Ascension Day. The wood may be lucky, but the flowers are not:

> Hawthorn bloom and elder flowers
> Fill the house with evil powers.

Black Fenland adders are often found curled in the elder's dry roots, and in the Fens its rank-smelling creamy flowers are said to attract snakes, although an anti-witch elder by the door is benign enough. In Somerset a wreath of flowers hung on the nearest ash tree to the farmhouse secures the household against snakebite for the year.

Garden flowers—daffodils, violets or lilac—with sweet smell and drooping heads, suggesting death, are unfortunate indoors, a belief which John Moore found lively in his Gloucestershire village in the 1950s, few venturing to bring a bowl of snowdrops into the house.[8] Holly flowers are ominous but the wood was valued by old builders for safeguarding doorsills and handles, and it is unlucky to fell a holly-tree near the house, as elsewhere.

An egg laid on Ascension Day, or a dried adder-skin in the rafters, and a houseleek growing on tiles or thatch, saved the house from fire, and acorn-shaped bobbins on window-blinds are reminders of the oak's ancient reputation as a deflector of lightning. The tree is rarely struck, but once when this occurred, in Needwood Forest, country people came miles to gather charred chips as firecharms. The orange-berried rowan, planted at northern cottage doors against witchcraft, is frequently seen in those parts of North America settled by Scots and Northcountrymen; when a Scottish settler at Chapman Camp, British Columbia, about 1936, planted three rowans at the doors of his house, he dourly refused to discuss his choice of tree, and neighbours' children were quickly reproved for swinging on them.[9] And sometime before 1893 Canon J. C. Atkinson watched a man hang two loops of rowan on Dr Alexander's house at Castleton, Yorkshire, and a third on the church gate, wheeling his horse a magical thrice before setting each charm against the evil eye.[10]

Like bees, houseplants are told of deaths; in Norfolk in 1926, Mrs C. M. Hood admired a fine geranium in a cottage window and was told that it had faded when the owner's father died, but had soon revived when properly put in mourning.[11] Generally a bird falling down the chimney or flying through a room is a death-omen. Wrens and robins are carefully protected and on Dartmoor house-fires and breakages of bones or crockery follow the destruction of nests. The country philosophy is expressed in a verse of 1770:

> I found a robin's nest within our shed,
> And in the barn a wren has young ones bred,
> I never take away their nest, nor try
> To catch the old ones, lest a friend should die.
> Dick took a wren's nest from his cottage side,
> And ere a twelvemonth past his mother dy'd![12]

'You won't want for luck now,' was a village comment when swallows settled at the writer's Buckinghamshire home in 1971, and a Suffolk clergyman wrote in 1860: 'Soon after setting up housekeeping for myself, I was congratulated on a martin having built its nest in the porch over the front door.'

Arthur Randell recalls his parents' horror when about 1909 he brought a young cuckoo home; he was ordered to return it to the nest forthwith, lest ill-luck enter the house. His parents took great care not to touch the bird themselves and his mother quickly brushed pungent herbs round the rooms to drive the devil away. Snakes are ominous about the house. About 1900 the writer's grandmother came out of her Sussex washhouse to find an adder curled up on the step enjoying the sun; she confessed afterwards that she knew this to be a death portent but added, 'Since the family was waiting for its dinner, I picked up my skirts and petticoats and jumped right over it!'

On cottage walls might hang the apocryphal medieval 'Our Saviour's Letter', supposedly written by Christ to Agbarus of Edessa and reprinted as a nineteenth-century broadsheet; it was known as far afield as Newfoundland and was particularly protective of women in childbirth.[13]

WASHING AND HOUSEWORK

Laundry, with overtones of purification and fresh beginnings, easily engendered folklore. Until at least the early twentieth century, little washing was done on 28 December, Childermas, undoubtedly the unluckiest day of the year, upon which many village churches rang a muffled peal, or on Good Friday, when the housewife might find washing spotted with Christ's blood. Today there is still reluctance in Devon to wash blankets in May or clothes on New Year's Day. 'Very few people in the village would do that now on either day. They say "Better be on the safe side" and great washdays take place in the weeks preceding May so that none need be done during the month or "one of the family may be washed away",' writes Miss Trump. A carelessly-ironed sheet or tablecloth showing a 'coffin' at the fold, suggests the early death of its user. Inherited linen and clothes are likely to wear badly, fretting for former owners, and new clothes washed for the first time at the new moon will be short-lived. Country housewives still spread stained tablecloths on the lawn on moonlit nights so that, by imitative magic, the moon's pale rays may whiten them.

A country washing-day

Especially as a new bride the housewife carefully swept dust inwards lest she sweep luck from the house and 'Sweep the house with blossomed broom in May, you'll sweep the head of the house away,' was widely believed. A broom, the housewife's emblem, intimated her absence from home and showed that her husband would welcome visits from his male friends to relieve his solitude. Dr Lucas recalled that his father, a physician in Burwell, Cambridgeshire during the 1850s, was once driving in Swaffham Bulbeck when he noticed brooms sticking from the window of a wine merchant's house. He investigated and was invited to join a large party of men enjoying wine in the parlour, while the merchant's wife was away.[14] Respectable Fenland housewives, however, never left a broom on view if they *were* at home, for it showed that a man's company would be welcome, a dangerous state of affairs if husbands were away, or the occupant of the house a widow without matrimonial ambitions. St Distaff's Day (7 January), when housework began after Christmas, is still an excellent day to turn out chests and cupboards in Devon, for no moths will then invade them. A bed turned on a Friday would turn away the bedmaker's sweetheart and in Oxfordshire it was said:

> If one day you would be wed
> Turn your bed from foot to head.

A St Mary Tavy, Devon, man remarked in 1850, 'My housemaid says she would not turn my bed on a Sunday on any account,' for nightmares would follow. A small ball of feathers or 'feather-luck' was thrust into a new bed for good fortune[15] and an inscribed wooden bed-smoother, often of *lignum vitae*, was a popular love-token, intended to prepare the bridal bed. When feather beds were in fashion housewives maintained that feathers lay more smoothly if the bed were turned at the moon's wane when her powers of attraction were least. A holed stone or knife and steel under the bed save the farmer from bad dreams[16] and a pillow stuffed with hops is still recommended for insomnia.

FIRE AND HEARTH

The hearth is the natural heart of the house, a family gathering-place, and in 1955 a correspondent wrote in *The Countryman* that as a child in Oxfordshire her maid's mother had taught her that the hearth was the 'altar of the house', to be kept spotless, a primitive idea expressed through gleaming blackleaded grates, whitened hearthstones and polished fire irons. The first instinctive act of many new owners of old cottages is to restore to their former importance evocative inglenook fireplaces with smoke-darkened bricks and beams.

John Aubrey found a hearth charm used in the seventeenth century at Quarrendon, Buckinghamshire, home of St Osyth: 'In those dayes, when they went to bed they did rake up the fire and make an + in the ashes, and pray to God and St Sythe to deliver them from fire and from water and from all misadventure.'[17] A cross is still marked on a new hearthstone in Somerset or made with iron in salt on hearth or oven to cure a smoking chimney. A poker laid across the grate-bars in cross-form draws up a stubborn fire and 'keeps Old Lob [the devil] from the hearth'. The writer's Sussex grandmother always did this, not for superstitious reasons she insisted, but because 'The metal draws the flame by dividing the draught.' In Leicestershire a horse-shoe lay in the fire against witches.

Faggots must contain at least thirteen sticks 'to burn Judas', but hedgers carefully omit elder—the wood of the cross, and that upon which Judas is said to have hung himself—from them. Older people still avoid elder as firewood, saying it will 'raise the devil'—probably meaning any one of a whole pantheon of ancient deities, rather than Satan specifically—or induce a death in the family, although some-times rationalising that the wood 'spits' in burning. To burn apple-wood is almost sacrilege; the tree is an ancient symbol of plenty and to destroy it might disturb the household's prosperity. As a child in Caterham, Surrey, about 1937, the writer well remembers the domestic unease when apple branches blown down in a gale were thriftily burned in the fireplace, although the sweet smoke was appreciated. Green ash wood is undoubtedly best for a hot, crackling fire:

> Burn ashwood green
> 'Tis fire for a queen

and Devon magic is suggested by Herrick's fire-lighting charm:

> Wash your hands, or else the fire
> Will not teend to your desire;
> Unwasht hands, ye Maidens, know,
> Dead the Fire, though ye blow.

KITCHEN LORE

The country housewife, mistress of the subtle arts of brewing, baking, dairy-work, preserving and ham-curing, cherished a rich store of traditional recipes for both everyday cookery and for the great feasts of Christmas, sheepshearing and harvest-home. She was ever reluctant to pass on her secrets for she might 'give away' her skills as well.

Breadmaking, symbol of life and redolent of the potent harvest spirit, was a milestone of the week. With natural movement, mystery and unpredictability, yeast is inevitably supportive of beliefs; it is said that a cross will be found on a bucket of yeast set to sponge on Good Friday and that a bun or loaf made entirely on that day has healing properties and, spiced or not, will never go mouldy. 'They only dries up,' said one baker. Such a bun, which will last a lifetime, makes a powerful kitchen charm. Only about twenty-five years ago a Herefordshire baker showed Mr H. L. V. Fletcher a hot cross bun still perfectly fresh in November, and invested in its maker's mind with special and incorruptible qualities.[18]

Dorset villagers hung a miniature loaf from Good Friday's baking at the fireside, for it would prevent other bakings from turning 'vinny' (mouldy) or sour. Ascension Day rainwater added to dough made loaves light, and a polished blackleaded fossilised sea-urchin or 'fairy-loaf' adorned Suffolk mantelpieces to cause the bread to rise in simulation of its own domed shape. Its presence ensured that the family would never lack bread. If wheat were harvested before it had hardened, the bread made from it would be fibrous and 'ropy'. Lincolnshire housewives then took care to 'gibbet the bread'—run a stick through the defective loaf and hang it in the cupboard as a charm to prevent a repetition of this calamity at later bakings.

Bread must not be burned or thrown away, and Alison Uttley in The Country Child tells how Susan Garland guiltily turned back two miles on her way home from school to pick up a crust she had heedlessly dropped, fearing, on reflection, that she would bring want on her family. Feeding birds with crumbs may well be a guilt-assuaging rather than a benevolent act. Kneading-trough, dough-kiver or tub, flour, sponge and dough, were marked with protective crosses or, in Somerset, with heart between crosses, and 'leavens laid' overnight were always treated thus, lest witches dance upon them. Only one person might reach into the oven during baking or quarrels would arise and irreverent singing was forbidden in the kitchen. If bread were cut on baking-day loaves would sink, and

> She that pricks bread with fork or knife
> Will never be happy, maid or wife.

A skewer must be used. Everywhere upturning a loaf was ominous: 'Home in Nova Scotia, I baked loaves of bread. When I tipped the pan to turn a loaf out upside down on the table, my grandmother snatched the loaf and quickly turned it over, saying reprovingly, "Never put a loaf upside down or a ship at sea will sink." '[19]

Beer, brewed regularly by many households until 1914, was also controlled by magical yeast. The heart and crosses charm on the mash or a live coal thrown into the vat, saved the brew from the fairies; in Shropshire a precautionary cross was made at every bunghole, while in Kent iron bars laid across casks kept beer from souring during thunderstorms. A saint beneficently influenced brewery, bakehouse and pigsty:

> The day of St Thomas, the blessed divine
> Is good for brewing, baking and killing fat swine.

October ale and 'key beer', the strongest brews, were kept locked in the farm cellar for obvious reasons. The 'howlt' or potency of home-brews merited respect and Devon horsemen were warned:

> Cider on beer, never fear.
> Beer on cider, makes a bad rider!

Great quantities of ale and cider were drunk on dusty harvest days and mulled in winter chimney-corners for heartening effect. Until this century, by old custom, each labourer who lived in the farmhouse had his own two-quart field keg or firkin, marked with his initials, filled by farmer or bailiff each morning and when not in use left on a nail by the cellar door.

Drifting china-pink and white apple-blossom marks the spring orchards of the cider-making counties of the West of England. A century ago every farm there made cider. *The Book of Days* noted that red and yellow apples were carefully gathered, laid in the warm September sun to mellow, and ground in creaking stonewheeled cidermills, worked by farmhorses. Commercial cider-makers still grow some of the old cider apples, among them Black Norman, Breakwell Foxwhelp, Fair Maid of Devon, Strawberry Norman, Barn Door, Harry Masters' Jersey and Slack-ma-Girdle—once prized in farm orchard and garden.[20] Homemade wines—cowslip, damson, elderberry, dandelion, parsnip and parsley (which in John Moore's Gloucestershire village has a considerable reputation as an aphrodisiac),[21] perry, passing in the early nineteenth century as champagne,[22] and mead, jewel-bright and fragrant—completed the country cellar.

English cookery is rich in pies, jams and preserves—gooseberry, plum, blackberry, quince and cherry among them—which with pickles and vinegars, bring zest to the table. Preserves were once made at the moon's prime to obtain the maximum yield from fruit, and forty years ago Somerset housewives marked a cross on each pot of jam to save it from shrinking, and stirred their boiling jam with a rowan or hazel stick so that fairies could not steal it.

Sagacious housewives safeguarded suet puddings (mainstays of the rural diet), with the sign of the cross, as they were committed to the pot. 'Pudding is so natural to our Harvest-men that without it they think they cannot make an agreeable dinner.'[23] The suetcrust Bedfordshire clanger or long dumpling, with meat, potatoes and onion at one end and jam at the other, made a handy meal for the fields ('dockey' in the Fens, 'nammit' or 'noonmeat' in Devon and Dorset, 'bait' in Wiltshire), carried to the harvest-field in a flat rush dinner-basket, hanging from the shoulder on a carefully polished harvest-stick. John Couzens told Parson Kilvert on Holy Thursday 1875, that he liked his bait crusty, so threw it down on the hayfield grass for the sun to 'bless' it to his liking. In Buckinghamshire, mid-morning bread, cheese and beer was 'baiver'. 'Twordunt blocked when we knocked off for baiver, wor it, Jack?' said one member of a Waddesdon threshing gang to Jackie Church, when the engine balked after the break. 'That it twordunt,' agreed Jack.[24] As late as 1936 the writer's Berkshire grandmother began Sunday dinner in old farming style with suet pudding served alone with gravy to take the edge from appetites when meat was short, and Mr Holbrook, the old-fashioned Cheshire farmer in Mrs Gaskell's *Cranford*, told Miss Matty that his father's rule was 'No broth, no ball, no ball, no beef'. Broth from the meat began the meal, suet pudding followed and then the joint itself.

Piecrusts, jams and sauces and boiling pots in general are still stirred sunwise, in a remnant of ancient sun-worship (even millstones ran with the sun and a 'left-handed' mill was a great rarity). Pastry marked with the charm of heart and crosses turned out light and crisp. North Country housewives silently dedicated to an absent person each string of black or white puddings[25] as it was dropped into the pot, and Somerset housewives begged an old wig from the parson to hang in the chimney during the cooking, both procedures to save the puddings from bursting. Before the Reformation, certain numbers of Ave Marias and Paternosters timed cooking operations and later housewives might say, 'I have made my pies all right, if only the Lord will be with them in the oven.'

Syllabub, a curd of warm milk made with port, sherry, cider or ale, according to county, was first favourite at any farm party. At Shapwick Marsh, Dorset, the 'feast of syllabub' was held about two weeks after the Marsh opened for grazing in June; owners of cows sent milk according to their means, Dr Heath (vicar 1805-22), gave wine, and the syllabub, made in milking-pails, was eaten after milking time. Mrs Rundell's recipe of 1835 for 'A very fine Somersetshire Syllabub' reads:

> In a large China Bowl put a pint of port, and a pint of sherry, or other white wine; sugar to taste. Milk the bowl full. In twenty minutes time cover it pretty high with clouted cream; grate over it nutmeg, put pounded cinnamon and non pariel comfits.

For best results the cow was milked straight into the wine, as at Shapwick and sometimes the dish was called 'hatted kit'—the 'kit' was the wooden milking-pail and the curd the 'hat'.

Pork was, to this century, the principal meat for country families of modest means, and beef and mutton were usually only eaten fresh on festive occasions, or dried during winter. Pig-killing was an important event, producing a dazzling array of cuts and dishes—critlings, chitterlings, flear, faggots, haseletts, muggerums, griskins, rearings, scratchings, trotters, brawn, sausages and black puddings as well as hams, bacon and pork pies for months to come. (At market pork pies wore sprigs of sage, mutton pies, sprigs of mint.) Afterwards neighbours attended the 'hog-feast' or received small presents of meat, called pleasantly 'pig-cheer'. Arthur Randell recalls that the event was 'a pig killed in the house'—one fattened at home—and in 1943 Walter Rose wrote reminiscently that few pig-killings passed without a bilious attack. Wise households killed only at the moon's waxing, or the meat would shrink in cooking, a belief still found today in England and North America, and no menstruating or pregnant woman must touch the meat: 'We took good care to keep the girls from it,' said a Buckinghamshire farmer, 'or it would spoil.' Thomas Ratcliffe of Worksop reported in 1878 that when he was sent a plate of 'pig's fry' by a cottage neighbour he was respectfully cautioned, 'Don't wash the plate, please, or the pig won't take the salt.'[26]

In 1826 it was still customary in some villages to kill beasts at Martinmas, the first day of winter, New Style, in an echo of the medieval practice when few animals were fed through the winter. Northumberland families clubbed together in a 'mart' to purchase an animal, and 'Martlemas beef' was beef dried like bacon in the chimney. Roast beef, on its rarer appearances, was accompanied by horse-radish sauce, and the old gardener at Kennel Moor maintained, even within the last thirty years, that the root's tang was keenest when it was dug at the full moon.[27]

'Buckinghamshire blacks'—local cherries with deep purple juice—are valued for pies and jam. Until World War I whole families walked into the Chiltern Hills to spend Cherry Pie Sunday in the open air, eating their pies and dozing in the sun,[28] and in 1923 W. R. Lethaby in *Home and Country Arts* said he could still trace the old cherry-harvest festival round Stokenchurch surviving 'as a sort of rivalry amongst the women in making cherry-turnovers'. Cherry 'bumpers' (large turnovers) are still sold at the August Cherry Pie Feast at the Plough Inn, Cadsden. 'Cherry pudden'—a suet pudding with cherries,

eaten with broad beans and boiled bacon—was another Buckinghamshire summer delicacy, and plum dumplings or 'heg-peg dumps' are
the traditional pudding at Nympsfield Feast in Gloucestershire on
St Margaret's Day. Warden pears, cooked whole in red wine, cinnamon and cloves, were cried at Bedford at the feast of St Simon and
St Jude on 28 October, and at Triscombe Revel on the last Sunday in
August Somersetshire whortleberry pickers assembled for the first
whort-pies and cream of the season and, for luck, to eat one pie between
every dance and song. Apple pies appear on every country table;
Yorkshiremen say 'An apple pie without some cheese, is like a kiss
without a squeeze', and visitors to pioneer North America noted that
there, too, apple pie was invariably eaten with cheese, as indeed it still is.

The finest Yorkshire pudding, for which the county's housewives
have the proverbial 'light hand', is made from magical 'beastings', the
first rich milk given by a cow after calving, thick and yellow as
double cream, and still sent by dairy farmer to valued friend, who must
return the jug unwashed, to bring luck to both herd and recipient.
Beastings (beestlings or bissons) makes a rich custard, and in Derbyshire golden curd-and-currant tarts.

Hundreds of 'feasten' and everyday cakes played their part in the
year's passage—Yorkshire parkin, Shrewsbury cakes, cowslip cake,
gilded gingerbread 'parliament' shapes—cats, clocks, royal arms,
'husbands' or flowers, wiggs, Cumberland currant pastry (with scratchings over from lard rendering), Devon revel buns (baked on sycamore
leaves) and cheesecakes, of which enough were eaten at the Whitsun-
tide feast at Melton Mowbray, it was said, to pave the whole town.

Fields and hedgerows offered many valuable plants; yellow lady's
bedstraw or cheese-rennet, for curdling milk and colouring cheeses
(especially in Cheshire), and making junkets; green nettletops with
which the floors of spotless dairies were scrubbed to raise the desired
growth of blue cheese moulds; juicy May elder shoots, from a protective tree left untouched in many farm gardens, which Mrs Rundell
in *A New System of Domestic Cookery*, 1835, recommended for 'an
English bamboo pickle'. The moon had a predictable influence over the
fugitive field delicacy of mushrooms, gleaming white among the fairy-
rings (in Sussex 'hag-tracks') of damp cow-pastures:

When the moon is in the full, mushrooms you may freely pull
But when the moon is on the wane, wait ere you think to pluck again.

Blackberries are picked before Michaelmas Day, when the 'devil spits on them'; Miss Trump remembers that Broad Clyst children passed blackberry bushes on the way to school; each chose a bush then taboo to the others, but all bushes were without restriction after 29 September. At Fontmell, Dorset, fifty years ago, children enjoyed a school holiday and families spent an autumn 'Nutting Day' in the green and bronze woods, opened by Sir Richard Glyn to his tenants. Storing foods underground was thought a particularly effective way of protecting them from the moon's disturbing influence. Nuts for Christmas were kept in this way, in earthenware crocks buried in the garden. At Ashmore, girls made special 'nutting dresses', but none dared to nut on Sunday lest the devil appear to hold her nutting bag, or, in accord with the nut-tree's fertility associations, she go pregnant to the altar. Riding between Worth, Sussex and Tunbridge Wells, on 30 August 1823, William Cobbett saw nuts clustering thickly on the late summer hedgerows and recalled that a good nut year was thought fruitful for bastards. A farmer, an experienced overseer of the poor, had once assured him that the belief was fully justified.

HOUSEHOLD FAIRIES

Domestic fairies—piskies, hobs or boggarts—intimately connected with daily work of farm and cottage, performed many useful tasks, if unpredictably, and were affectionately regarded by their fortunate hosts. Before the advent of threshing machines a Cornish farmer was surprised by the great quantity of corn mysteriously threshed the previous night. He peeped into the barn by moonlight and saw a small fellow in a shabby green suit threshing faster than the eye could see, and crept away, debating how best to show his gratitude. New clothes, he decided, were a practical gift and accordingly a small suit was left in the barn. Again the farmer watched; the pisky put on the suit, looked at himself admiringly, crying 'Pisky fine and pisky gay, pisky now will fly away,' and from that time on no further help was received from the fairy flail. Many were the stories of piskies, however obliging, driven away by gifts of clothes. As late as 1867, Syke Lumb Farm, near Blackburn, Lancashire, was the home of a boggart who in good humour would milk cows, pull hay, harness horses, and stack crops. But if it were vexed by some imaginary slight, cream-mugs were smashed, butter would not come, horses were unable to move empty carts across the farmyard and cows were driven to the woods, or chained unwillingly two to one stall—while the goblin sat on a cross-beam of the barn, grinning with delight at the confusion. Sometimes the farmer's family fared no better, for bedclothes were pulled off and the unlucky sleepers dragged downstairs in great discomfort.

Fairies were enemies of sluttishness, a reputation doubtless fostered by careful housewives to encourage their maids:

> If ye will with *Mab* find grace,
> Set each Platter in his place:
> Rake the Fier up, and get
> Water in, ere Sun be set.
> Wash your Pailes, and clense your Dairies;
> Sluts are loathsome to the Fairies:
> Sweep your house: Who doth not so,
> *Mab* will pinch her by the toe.

A Staffordshire woman at a farm near Mixon, spoke of Old Nancy, a fairy 'who had been about there since goodness knows when' and who made her kindly presence known by rapping on the wainscot panelling as the fire burned low late in the evening. Her mother had counselled her to be good to the fairies; for a piece of cake and a bottle of home-brewed ale they might be relied upon to find lost iron plough-pins and prevent hedgehogs sucking the cows during the night-time. Their little tobacco pipes were found about the fields and the ploughman who found one was 'lucky'.[29]

Fairies were generally welcome and about 1850 a cottager near Polyphant, Cornwall, explained that he left a hole in his housewall unrepaired, 'on purpose for the piskies to come in and out, as they had done for many years'. By the mid-nineteenth century the old confident belief was fading, though Thomas C. Couch, writing about 1852, noted that it was far from dead—one old lady exclaimed pettishly to a doubting visitor, 'What! Not believe in 'em, when my poor mother had been pinched black and blue by 'em!'—'though people of the present generation hold it by a slighter tenure than their forefathers did, and are aware that piskies are *now* fair objects of ridicule, whatever they formerly were.'[30]

THE FAMILY BEES

Until the twentieth century bees were widely thought to be intelligent creatures of mystery and prediction, useful to man, aligned with his personal fortunes and worthy of confidences. Their model industry and domestic harmony seemed a reflection of all a household should be. The bond between owner and bees was strong, and astute old countrymen claimed to be able to recognise their own bees when they met them at work in field and hedgerow. In both England and North America bees were punctiliously told of family happenings: 'About 1900, near Hastings,' writes Mrs Baker, 'I saw an old lady moving purposefully round her hives, lips moving silently. I was told she was "telling her bees".' Another writer remembers tying white ribbons to the hives on her Aunt Jenny's wedding-day and it was said that on this occasion one bee even went to church on the bride's bouquet,[31] while a swarm on the wedding-day was an excellent omen. But most important of all, bees must be told of deaths, or they too would die. In Worcestershire the family nurse padded out to tap the straw bee-skeps under the apple trees with the house-key and say 'Your master's dead but don't you go, your mistress will be a good mistress to you,' and the bees would hum to show their approval of a new owner. From Sussex to Maryland, beekeepers took care to give this news before sunrise on the following day. Even today these beliefs and practices are not quite obsolete.

After a North Lincolnshire death about 1850, an old lady asked if the bees had been told. No one seemed certain, but she maintained that if this had been forgotten, they would desert the hives. 'Some people give them a piece of the funeral cake,' she went on, 'I don't think this is absolutely necessary, but certainly it *is* better to tell them of the death.' This done, the bees began to work again and everyone agreed it was because they had been properly informed. Funeral-feast cake and wine, a taste of everything on the table, was left by the hives, and in the parish of Ecclesfield about 1855 the Rev Alfred Gatty found the old practice of formally inviting the bees to funerals still observed. Such traditional observances did not always go smoothly, as an account of 1790 noted:

A superstitious custom prevails at every funeral in Devonshire, of turning round the bee-hives that belonged to the deceased, if he had any, and that at the moment the corpse is carrying out of the house. At a funeral some time since, at Cullompton, of a rich old farmer, a laughable circumstance of this sort occurred: for, just as the corpse was placed in the hearse, and the horsemen, to a large number, were drawn up in order for the procession of the funeral, a person called out, 'Turn the bees', when a servant who had no knowledge of such a custom, instead of turning the hives about, lifted them up, and then laid them down on their sides. The bees, thus hastily invaded, instantly attacked and fastened on the horses and their riders. It was in vain they galloped off, the bees as precipitately followed, and left their stings as marks of their indignation. A general confusion took place, attended with loss of hats, wigs &c., and the corpse during the conflict was left unattended; nor was it till after a considerable time that the funeral attendants could be rallied, in order to proceed to the interment of their deceased friend.[32]

Until the eighteenth century, honey was the principal sweetener in the kitchen and figured in ham-curing and preserving of all kinds. It was taken, wallflower-dark, in pendulous yellow combs shaped like the rounded straw bee-skeps from which they had come, and dripped into earthenware 'pancheons' for bottling. The wax made polish, candles and medicines, and it was wise to remember to thank the bees for their gifts.

Knowing old beemasters professed to detect a change in the note of the bees' humming just before swarming, and the occurrence was full of omens. When a Suffolk swarm was taken from the household pump by the coachman, someone commented on the cheapness of the bees acquired, but a servant remarked gloomily that if the rightful owner did not claim the swarm a family death would follow within the year. Within living memory 'tanging' was thought to make a flying swarm settle. *Tusser Redivivus*, 1744, noted: 'The tinkling after them with a warming pan, frying pan, kettle, is of good use to let the neighbours know you have a swarm in the air, which you claim whenever it lights . . .' Some felt themselves immune from charges of trespass, for a right was created when 'tanging', and sometimes the shovel used to beat the tattoo marked the claim while the owner ran home for a skep. Country people still believe that aromatic herbs such as lemon balm (bee balm), lavender and thyme rubbed on hives will detain a flying swarm. Random placing of hives about orchard and garden is explained by the tradition that wherever a swarm settles —under thatched eaves, in apple-boughs or deep among gooseberry bushes—there, on the nearest open ground, must the hive be placed.

Bees participated in the seasonal feasts; in Devon they received a 'handsel' of honey and sugar on New Year's Day and hummed the Old Hundredth psalm on Old Christmas Day (owners of bees crept into the garden to listen). Dorset beekeepers examined their hives on Good Friday and strewed protective salt on the floors.

Selling bees was a delicate matter which must not imply disrespect; to barter a bushel of corn or a small pig for the hive might be advisable or, if money *were* offered, a gold coin was correct:

> If you wish your bees to thrive,
> Gold must be paid for every hive;
> For when they're bought with other money,
> There will be neither swarm nor honey.

So said Sussex beekeepers. Bees never thrived in a quarrelsome family and when he noticed deserted hives in a Suffolk garden, an enquiring vicar was told: 'Them bees couldn't du. There was *words* about them . . .'

THE POULTRY YARD

Setting eggs is a critical act with overtones of fertility rituals and number taboos. Until the late nineteenth century it was thought unwise to carry fertile hens' eggs over running water, or to set them on a Sunday or in May, the month of witchcraft. Spring flowers adversely affected hatching and if less than thirteen primroses were brought into the house as a spring posy, so many eggs would each hen hatch. About 1852 a Norfolk parson told that one of his first duties on arrival in his parish had been to separate two quarrelling old women, one of whom accused the other of maliciously giving a neighbour's child a single primrose to take home, to cause the hens, by imitative magic, to hatch only one egg each. Like produced like; each primrose represented a yellow chick and while a large bunch of primroses could do no harm (for a hen could hardly hatch too many chicks), a smaller

A safe vase of primroses for the house

bunch would induce less than the traditional brood. Violets and snowdrops had a similar effect and Manx and Somerset farmers' wives never brought daffodils into the house until the geese had safely hatched their eggs, lest they see the yellow flowers, mistake them for goslings and desert their nests.

It is still widely believed in rural England and the United States that only an odd number of eggs should be set, at the moon's increase for numerical success, and at sunset (or in Maryland at high tide) for pullets. Housewives passed a lighted candle over, or pencilled crosses on, the newly-set clutch, to save it from foxes and weasels. The last egg laid by an old hen was kept as a fertility charm of continuity, while a white pullet's first egg, a charm of anticipation, was the luckiest present for a country sweetheart; the small 'runt' or 'witch' egg was ill-omened and the hen laying it was killed. Elder is a poor shade-tree for poultry and farmers' wives rejected its wood (although white, easily cut and close-grained) for poultry skewers, because, they maintained, its rank odour tainted flesh, but probably acknowledging the tree's ancient association with witchcraft. From Lincolnshire to Tennessee it was unlucky to bring eggs into the house after sunset, and the *Stamford Mercury*, 29 October 1852, mentioned another belief. A visitor had called at an East Markham farmhouse a few days before to buy eggs. The farmer's wife had agreed that she had a few score to sell and the customer said, 'Then I'll take them home with me in the cart,' to receive the indignant response, '*That* you'll not! Don't you know the sun has gone down? You're welcome to the eggs at a proper hour of the day; but I would not let them go out of the house after the sun is set on any consideration whatever!'

'Whistling maid and crowing hen, is neither good for God nor men,' and Arthur Randell writes that no Fenman would dream of keeping a hen with this not-unusual characteristic, since sexual abnormality, if not swiftly countered, may adversely affect the fortune of the whole community. About 1966 he had killed such a hen for neighbours and their luck quickly improved.

THE GARDEN

Gardening lore reflects the superiority in the countryman's eyes of vegetables and herbs over flowers. Potatoes, peas and beans planted on Good Friday are certain to thrive, for Satan's power over the soil is then suspended. In Devon they say 'We sow our potatoes at the foot of the cross,' and Somerset beans sown on Good Friday will 'rise on Easter Day with Christ'. Good Friday was once one of the countryman's rare holidays and also at a suitable time for spring planting, adding pragmatism to mysticism. Nova Scotia cabbage plants set on Good Friday, and in Kentucky on any Friday at the new moon, are safe from frost. Mr Christopher D. Sansom writes (1973) from Kennel Moor, near Godalming, Surrey, that at Easter 1955 his father suggested to a gardener there that he would presumably wish to be free over the Easter weekend. The man declined the offer, saying that he wanted to carry out spring sowings of various seeds on the day after Good Friday, 'while the Master's body lay on the ground'.[33]

Other dates in the church's calendar had beneficial effects on planted seeds, and Robert Bond told John Brand of a belief he had found round Gloucester that seeds planted on Palm Sunday would yield double flowers. Sometimes Good Friday sowing at noon precisely was advised for the production of double gillyflowers (a term embracing stocks, clove-scented pinks or wallflowers), and about 1858 Canon C. W. Bingham wrote that he had received from a Dorset cottage garden a Brompton stock whose excellence was attributed to Good Friday planting. Saints' days were also well liked; before calendars were common, they combined a useful reminder of the date with the hope that the saint's benign aura might benefit germination. St Patrick's Day, 17 March, was the Cheshire choice for potato-setting; Candlemas Day, New or Old Style (St Valentine's Day), a cross-quarter day in the Celtic calendar, was favourable for all seeds, and within living memory Buckinghamshire and Somersetshire gardeners planted shallots and beans on St Thomas's Day, 21 December, at the winter solstice, from which days steadily lengthen to summer.

Apart from saintly influence, sympathetic magic easily suggests that seeds planted then will similarly increase with daylight hours, and in accord with this doctrine harvesting should be done on the longest day, at the summer solstice, magically emblematic of maximum growth and size in crops. In the last century, Lancashire gardeners favoured St Gregory the Great's Day, 12 March ('Gregory-gret-onion') for onion-setting, and Cecil Atkins remembers that, typical of local rules in many districts, Ashendon Feast Day, the second Tuesday in May, is correct for bean-planting round Waddesdon. Similarly 'Dunnifer' or Dunningworth fair day is the day for spring-cabbage sowing in the Blaxhall district of Suffolk. (Reminders could be reversed. An old Sussex man told William Wood, author of *A Sussex Farmer*, 1938, 'Ah, Easter Sunday, that's the first Sunday after the first full moon after you put your onions in.') Leaf size was a sure guide:

> When the elum leaves are as big as a farden,
> 'Tis time to plant kidney beans in the garden,

referring to the now obsolete farthing, a small copper coin. Mrs A. F. Smith of Patchway, Bristol, recalls that over sixty years ago her father always planted his kidney beans in rows running from north to south, to ensure a good crop.[34] Rural beliefs concerning north-to-south positioning, anciently based upon the importance of the Pole Star and reverence for the earth's magnetic forces, now seem to encompass the overtly superstitious and the practical. Yorkshire farmers placed drying corn stooks from north to south and garden rows were planted thus, so that either side would enjoy equal exposure to sun. Purely superstitious is the Cambridgeshire belief that parsley seed, notoriously reluctant to germinate, should be sown at the new moon in north–south alignment, achieved by night sowing with the Pole Star and Plough (the Dipper in North America) as guides.

In garden sowing, as on the farm, the moon's phases were of significance. Mrs Evelyne E. Bowes told the writer in 1973 that her father, 'a wonderful gardener', who had died recently aged 92, always considered the moon's phase before planting. The first quarter was the favoured time, especially for kidney beans: 'Never plant too soon, consult the moon,' was his advice. He was once gardener to a titled lady fond of Parma violets, and on one occasion was replanting the second of two frames of these flowers when a solar eclipse occurred. The violets planted before the eclipse were satisfactory, but those in the second frame remained so stunted that they were finally pulled out and burned, all felt to be in accord with the East Anglian belief that 'Everything in the garden stands still during an eclipse.'[35]

Miss Trump writes of a planting belief in her Devon village earlier this century. Squire Were, 'rather a stern old gentleman, white-bearded', would at the cuckoo's first spring call send his man to plant the French beans immediately, linking practicality with the magical reappearance of this bird of summer. Somerset gardeners still mark a cross on the earth when spring planting is completed, and until the last century Herefordshire seedbeds were spiked with rowan and birch crosses on May morning. As a child Miss Ruth Tongue remembers making the charm sign, heart between crosses, with the stick offered her (probably hazel), by a Somerset cottager, on the newly-turned soil of his garden. She has since seen the sign once or twice more, tucked in a quiet corner of a farm garden and intended to keep the fairies away.

The sweet-scented beanflower is associated with death and the appearance of a white bean in a row still disturbs some country gardeners. Even to sniff the flowers may be ill-advised. Marking a cross on the stalk of any cabbage cut, to encourage the growth of young greens for the winter table, could well be a rationalisation of a superstitious practice.

Transplanting parsley except on Good Friday is dangerous; a family death, especially that of the gardener, may follow. Today country people still give the plant away reluctantly, although an applicant may safely help himself. In Ontario the taboo extended even to offering thanks for the cuttings, however obtained. Parsley grows best for, variously, the wicked, the honest or 'where the old grey mare is the better horse'. It germinates slowly, and 'visits Satan nine times' or 'goes to hell and back' before appearing, although Good Friday sowing offsets delay. Boiling water (perhaps offensive to the Evil One) poured on the seed in the ground, produces germination in three instead of six weeks.[36]

Sage prospers for the wise, or again where petticoats rule, and as late as 1948 a North Oxfordshire man, fearing neighbours' laughter, chopped down a flourishing sagebush for:

> If the sagebush thrives and grows,
> The master's not master and he knows.

Rosemary lives for thirty-two years, the traditional age of Christ.[37] Rue flourishes if stolen; 'Sow fennel, sow trouble' is an old saying, p rhaps because of the inhibiting effect this herb has on other plant growth, but dill has a benign anti-witch reputation. An elderly Buckinghamshire villager insisted on taking her bay tree with her when she moved a few yards to a new home in 1968, or 'good luck would be left behind'.

In Guernsey watering with urine was advised for sweet, red apples,[38] and Staffordshire gardeners water prize chrysanthemums with the urine of a pregnant woman, now mundanely said to contain beneficial chemicals but perhaps a shadow of a primitive fertility belief. An informant remembers that when he, as a child in about 1944, was 'caught short' in his aunt's garden at Wembley, she always sent him to the runner beans, for urine was 'good for them'.[39] Pennsylvanian Dutch settlers in the United States horsewhipped their peach trees before breakfast on Good Friday to encourage fruiting and an old English saying similarly advised:

> A woman, a steak and a walnut tree,
> More you beat 'em, better they be.

Christopher Gullett in *Philosophical Transactions*, 1772, noted that turnips, cabbages, fruit trees and corn whipped with witch-repellent elder twigs would be safe from blight.

Hydrangeas, introduced into England in 1756, were late to attract folklore, but (particularly if blue-flowered) they are unlucky near or in the house and while they bloom daughters will not marry. Lilacs mourn and do not flower if one of their number is felled; pungent geraniums on the windowsill repel flies and myrtle is the luckiest plant for a window-box, laying a mantle of domestic happiness over the household. Scarlet poppies, linked with sleep and death, are ominous (in Buckinghamshire they are 'blindeyes', in Huntingdonshire 'headaches'). The prudent do not touch them. Pure white madonna lilies (which only grow for a 'good woman') keep ghosts from the house with their holy aura, and their free blooming once marked a year when corn would be plentiful and bread cheap. In Cambridgeshire the mauve periwinkle is the most fortunate plant for the newly-weds' garden. To pick pansies (provocatively called 'kiss-me-at-the-garden-gate' or 'tittle-my-fancy') with dew on them caused rain, and 'plucked poppies make thunder'. Lilies of the valley only thrive with Solomon's seal—'their husbands'—nearby.[40]

One expert rosegrower always advised 'Put a dead cat under them

Page 85 (above) Blessing the blossoms on the Old Mission Peninsula, Traverse City, Michigan, at the opening of the National Cherry Festival;

(centre) child's boots, dating from about 1840, found during the demolition of a cottage at Stanwick, Northamptonshire. Now in Northampton Museum;

(below) Goathland Plough Stots in a North Yorkshire village. The dancers hold swords aloft. At the right stands Auld Isaac, Betty with besom broom, the Gentleman and veiled Lady

Page 86 (*above*) Weighing an entry; a tense moment at the Egton Bridge Old Gooseberry Show. In 1952 Mr Tom Ventress entered a legendary gooseberry weighing nearly two ounces; (*below*) Morris dancers in traditional costume on the rectory lawn, Waddesdon, Buckinghamshire, on 9 July 1908. A photograph by Albert C. Cherry, the village photographer

—*then* you'll get some roses'; in Yorkshire at lamb-docking time a tail was buried under every newly-planted poplar tree and when ash trees were felled in the parish of Scotton, Lindsey, Lincolnshire about 1877, a horseshoe was found under each. A Suffolk farmer reported recently that when walnut trees are felled in his district gold coins are discovered among their roots and small pieces of coal are found directly under old perry-pear trees grubbed up in Gloucestershire, too frequently for the occurrence to be accidental.[41] These practices suggest recollections of primitive sacrifices to trees and plants.

Cottage gardens inspired a pleasant usage. In 1875 old Benjamin Hawkins told Parson Kilvert that when he was young, garden ground was precious and vegetables to feed the family had to take first place. But the old cottage women managed to have a flowerbed and grew fragrant pinks and roses, thyme and lads' love (or southernwood), which they made into nosegays bought by the village boys for a halfpenny each and worn in their hats on Sundays. From Rutland in 1879 Cuthbert Bede wrote to *Notes and Queries*: 'The country custom of wearing flowers at church is very general and I occasionally see them carried in the hand by girls.' The practice continued until at least 1910, for an informant from Swanton Novers told in *Within Living Memory; A Collection of Norfolk Reminiscences*, 1972, how his mother sold fruit and flowers from the garden to help the family income. Many a young man called on a Sunday morning to buy a buttonhole and a particular favourite was a bud from the rose Gloire de Dijon, which grew upon the wall.

Village flowershows are important country occasions, at which, in dim tents amid scents of sweetpeas and crushed grass, reputations have been made and marred. Speaking of the shows round Battle about 1900, Mrs Baker writes: 'There was great competition among the head gardeners on the estates at flowershow time. They were expected to grow the most exotic things—my father, Robert Aitken, grew melons, oranges, peaches, grapes and nectarines, as well as many flowers—and one estate provided horse transport to carry the cherished exhibits to the show.' Gardening competitions have been held in less formal circumstances. During World War II, gifts of 'beefsteak' tomato seed (familiar in North America but almost unknown in

England) were sent by the United States to English gardeners. Vast in their native land and even more spectacular in the soft airs and rich soil of England, the legendary tomatoes soon stimulated contests. At the Fuller's Arms, Brightling, Sussex, for example, the best tomatoes were weighed in the bar parlour every Saturday night and a prize given for the heaviest of the week. Gooseberry contests are a feature of North of England rural life; at Egton Bridge in the Esk Valley, a show is held on the first Tuesday in August in continuation of a long tradition, for the Egton Bridge Old Gooseberry Society was founded in 1800 and gooseberries have been grown round the village for 250 years. Rules are strict; no new member may compete using another's bushes, unless both belong to the same family, and even then transfers are carefully superintended by committee witnesses.[42]

4

The Country Calendar

The village calendar moved with the seasons—Christmas, Plough
Monday frolics, sports of Shrovetide, joys of Easter, May Day and
Midsummer and the gaiety of the autumn fairs, with their mumming,
morris-dancing, bonfires and merriment—all brought activities keenly
anticipated before the event, relished during it, and hallowed in fireside
memory.

CHRISTMAS

Christmas customs, the blazing yule-log, great meals and evergreens,
belong to the winter solstice, that welcome moment on 21 December
when the sun, the true country god of life, begins to climb the sky and
turn the year towards summer and green leaves. Once, the way of life
changed completely from Christmas Day to Twelfth Night—'I speak
not here of England's twelve dayes madness . . .';[1] the oxen rested in
their shed while 'Every Gentleman Feasted the Farmers, and every
Farmer their Servants and Task Men.'[2] Richard Blakeborough wrote
of his Yorkshire home in 1898:

> Our greatest observance of custom is, as it should be, in connexion with
> Christmas-tide, indeed, preparation for the same really commences some
> weeks in advance. There is the pudding to make and partly boil; all the
> ingredients for the plum-cake to order; the mincemeat to prepare for the
> mince-pies; the goose to choose from some neighbouring farmer's stock;
> the cheese to buy; and the wheat to have hullins beaten off and to cree, for

89

the all-important frumenty; the yule-cake or pepper-cake to make; the hollin to gather . . .[3]

It was widely believed until at least the end of the nineteenth century, that cattle knelt and perhaps spoke at midnight on Christmas Eve. Many had seen them. Parson Kilvert wrote on 5 January 1878 of James Meredith, noted for truthfulness, who at Staunton-on-Wye had watched cattle kneeling on Old Christmas Eve with tears flowing down their faces. A Nova Scotia farmer heard his oxen say, 'Tomorrow we'll be drawing wood to make our master's coffin,' and was so shocked that he died the next day. Even in 1928 no one visited the cattle on this farm on Christmas Eve—they were fed in the afternoon for safety's sake.[4]

As midnight approached all looked for the dark-haired male—the 'lucky-bird'—who, sprig of greenery in hand, 'let Christmas in'. In

Yorkshire children about 1860 singing carols on Christmas morning

Lancashire, a welcoming penny lay by the fire for him. A visitor to the North Riding in 1810 was pleasantly awakened at six o'clock on Christmas morning by sweet singing, and looking sleepily down into the dark garden saw a group of men and women carolling to welcome the day. Washington Irving, during his Yorkshire visit of 1820, wrote that such sounds 'as they receded, became more soft and aerial, and seemed to accord with quiet and moonlight'. At Chaddleworth, high among the Berkshire downs, the village waits, with fiddles, oboes, serpents and clarinets, snowflakes sparkling in the soft yellow light of their lanterns, sang when all were in bed; and in Somerset, 'holly riders', with berry-wreathed hats, rode round the hill-farms on stout Exmoor ponies, singing carols for cakes, cider and pennies. At Montacute the cellist accompanying the singers tuned his strings to one of the six bells, and at Ruarden, Gloucestershire, an Elizabethan benefactor left five shillings to pay for the ringing of a two-hour 'virgin peal' to welcome Christmas.

Yule-log and Evergreens

Symbol of country Christmasses, dragged home in triumph from the wintry woods, the decorated yule-log blazed and crackled on the hearth typifying warmth, light and cheer. Anyone meeting the merry procession raised his hat in salute, for the sight was full of good omens. Richard Blakeborough wrote: 'The days speed on, until there comes a night when the charred remains of last year's Yule log, glows with heat intense beneath the one of that year's cutting; for the new log must always rest upon and be lighted by the old one, which has been carefully stored away, for this, the night of nights—Christmas Eve.'[5] Northern farmhouse servants chose a slow-burning log, for while it burned they had ale and cider with their meals; the custom was carried to the southern United States by English settlers and the slaves searched the woods for the greenest logs they could find to prolong festivities.

From Newfoundland, where its lighting at sunset on Christmas Eve was marked by the cheerful firing of muskets or seal guns at every door,[6] to Sussex, the yule-log was a part of Christmas. It still burns at Colonial Williamsburg, Virginia and at the Empress Hotel, Victoria, British Columbia, where before Christmas dinner, watched by guests from all over North America, a procession forms of seneschal, jester, trumpeter and spirits of mirth in Elizabethan dress, with serving men carrying the yule log. 'Here We Come a-Wassailling' is sung and the log is proclaimed: 'I charge the log that it shall burn brightly and well on the wide hearth of this hospitable mansion, shedding a glow of warmth and friendliness . . .', and lighted with a 'splinter saved from a log of bygone year'—just as Robert Herrick had ordained in 1648.[7]

In the farms and inns of Devon and Somerset the log's place was taken by the ashen faggot, bound with nine withes and lighted with charred twigs from last year's Christmas hearth. The bursting of each band called for a quart of cider and toasts were drunk while the company jumped in sacks and ducked for apples and the great yule candle (which must be a gift and was often presented by the family's chandler) lighted at the dinner-table by the master of the house, burned steadily through the night.

The ashen faggot still burns in West Country inns, but Mr D. St Leger-Gordon believed that for some years before 1950 his had been the only household in his Dartmoor village where it still blazed on Christmas Eve, although he remembered the time where everywhere the green twigs had roared and exploded like gunshots as the music of the handbell ringers echoed round farmhouse kitchens. In 1878 the Devonshire Association found that the Christmas ashen faggot was burning at thirty-two farms and cottages in the Ashburton postal district alone.

Holly, a male emblem, brings fortune and fertility to the household. 'Holly be a man' and ivy, of clinging habit, is the feminine symbol. The Holly Boy and Ivy Girl are still remembered at Christmas. 'Must have a bit of "Christmas",' say villagers as they cut their holly, ritually breaking the usual taboo on touching it. Sterile holly is dangerous to farmer and stock alike, and in a poor berry year it is wise to put a sprig of ivy (perhaps with berries reddened with 'raddle' left over from sheep-marking) in the Christmas wreath as an antidote. The earliest day when holly or mistletoe may safely enter the house (and then only with a man) is Christmas Eve, and holly is kept and burned under next year's Christmas pudding, as a charm of continuity.

Precursor of the Christmas tree, the old English kissing-bough, a globe of evergreens looped with ribbons and baubles with shining red apples, and in recognition of the name, mistletoe slowly revolving below in the candles' draught, still hangs in northern cottages. During the making it hung from a hook, but never the one upon which it would later hang, which was sacred to the finished bunch.

On Holly Night at Brough, Westmorland, on Twelfth Night, the townspeople tied torches to every branch of a holly (later an ash; both were significantly magical trees) carried in procession by the local strong man, Joseph Ling. Cheers rang out, flambeaux blazed and fireworks roared up into the sky, before the tree's burned fragments were thrown to the crowd to be carried off to the inns. By Twelfth Night all decorations must be removed from houses and by 1 February, Candlemas Eve, the end of the ecclesiastical Christmas season, from churches also, or bad luck will follow. Superstitious

Holly Night at Brough

93

people sent servants to sweep private pews, lest a stray leaf be over-looked:

> ... For look how many leaves there be
> Neglected there (maids trust to me),
> So many *Goblins* you shall see.

All evergreens (excepting mistletoe which was kept in farmhouses in Worcestershire against the evil eye) must be burned out of doors, and in the United States the custom of burning household decorations in parks has grown, in compliance with the old belief.

Master and man dined together on Christmas Day after visiting stable and cowshed with special feeds. In Cumberland, every horse and cow had a 'Christmas sheaf' in its stall and sometimes another was nailed to the barn roof for the birds; Cheshire hens had double measures of grain, and observance of these rituals ensured a lucky year for the animals. Herefordshire farmer John Hughes sat down with his guests in 1796 to enjoy roast and boiled beef, hams, hares, geese and fowls, mince and apple pies, junkets, cinnamon cakes, cider cakes and Christmas cakes. New beer, and honey, primrose, elderberry and dandelion wines, made the party merry but even after these preparations John's anxious young wife set aside a big ham and rabbit pies lest country appetites exceed her preparations.[8] Cumberland farmers arranged two feasts for neighbours—'t'ould foaks neet' for the married and 't'young foaks neet' for the single, at which 'there was no distinction of persons,' a correspondent told William Hone in 1827 with satisfaction.

Sometimes a miniature wheatsheaf of gleaned corn hung from the kitchen rafters ready for Christmas frumety, which Richard Blakeborough noted in 1898 was always eaten at Yorkshire country Christ-masses; once finished on New Year's Eve, no more was made until the following year. In 1972, eighty years later, his son, Major J. Fairfax-Blakeborough, told the writer that frumety is still made for his North Riding home, from wheat prepared by the miller, directly descended from he who ground corn for the monks of Fountains Abbey. In Suffolk frumenty was set outside the door for the 'farisees' or fairies. Yule cakes of flour, yeast, raisins, currants, lemon peel and nutmeg, as large as a dinner plate and three inches thick, criss-crossed with a pastry network, were taken in Yorkshire, with a glass of mulled ale or hot elderberry wine and a slice from the great Wensleydale cheese, upon which a cross was scraped; in Derbyshire their accompaniment was the Christmas sage cheese, brilliant with spinach juice and the chopped herb. In Warwickshire cottages, a showy vegetable marrow which had hung, decorated with ribbons, from a beam since autumn, was stuffed and eaten at Christmas.

In Sussex the Christmas pudding was made on 'Stir-Up Sunday'. It was stirred sunwise 'three times three' with a wooden spoon (recalling the wooden manger) and as the family stirred, in decreasing order of seniority, they wished three times, although only one wish would be granted. The pudding was put aside to await the return of absent persons. Three was a pagan luck-bringing number, later linked with Trinity and Three Kings. Thirteen ingredients, in memory of Christ and his disciples, were allowed for both pudding and mincemeat, and thirteen puddings were made, 'one for every month and one for Judas'; Judas's pudding was quietly put aside to moulder, or given to a gipsy or tramp who might call over Christmas. A little finely chopped mutton or mutton suet was added to mince pies in remembrance of the shepherds of Bethlehem although beef was the more usual ingredient. In Nottinghamshire farmhouses about 1850 the family was given 'mince-pigs', 'the bigger the better', with long snouts, curling tails and crimped backs, and currants for eyes.[9] Mincemeat must be tasted by all—'every mincepie eaten away from home means a happy month to come'; but pies, made in twelves to strengthen the charm, must be offered by a friend. The ritual sampling and sharing of Christmas good things in as many houses as possible (and the frequent preservation of part of the Christmas cake for twelve months) expressed the hope of plenty for all in the coming year.

THE POOR

To within living memory, on 21 December, St Thomas's Day (Mumping, Gooding, Corning or Thomassing Day), poor people begged money and provisions for Christmas. Even in 1942, wrote Walter Rose of Haddenham, one old lady went 'a-Thomassing' in the village, more in affection for an old custom than from indigence.[10] Kindly Herefordshire farmers added a quartern measure of corn to the gleaners' pickings from the autumn fields, and this was ground free by the miller for Christmas loaves. Those who gave to the mumpers received sprigs of evergreen. On Gooding Day grocers in Taunton, Somerset, in the spirit of the old custom, gave complimentary goods and calendars to cheerful country shoppers in from the villages by gig or on horseback.

Wassaillers[11] were about the villages during the holiday, carrying great wooden bowls with arching iron bands decorated with evergreens and ribbons, and filled with 'lamb's wool'—hot ale, roasted crab apples, toast, nutmeg, sugar and eggs—steaming fragrantly in the wintry air. Offering their bowl to all whom they met, they sang:

> Wassail! Wassail! All over the town,
> Our toast it is white, our ale it is brown,
> Our bowl it is made of the maplin tree,
> We be good fellows, I drink to thee.

Yorkshire wassaillers carried little boxes with Advent images, the Virgin Mary, Holy Child and Three Kings, amid evergreens, with tinsel, an apple and an orange representing the gifts. Donors were given a flower or leaf from the box for luck—or as a sovereign charm against toothache. So unfortunate was it to be missed by the singers that a nineteenth-century phrase in Yorkshire was 'as unhappy as a man who has seen no Advent images.' Wassailling is in village pasts, but one group, led by Harold Tozer, who has wassailled for over sixty years, carries the traditional bowl, decorated with mistletoe and ribbons, to inns and farms round Truro, in Cornwall, just as the exiled Cornish miners did in nineteenth-century Butte, Montana.[12]

Crataegus monogyna 'Biflora', a variety of the common hawthorn, blooms in both winter and spring and the belief that it flowers about Christmas Day is well supported in fact, although much depends on the season.[13] The most famous example of this thorn was supposedly struck from the staff of St Joseph of Arimathea at Glastonbury, Somerset. On the eve of 25 December 1752, thousands with lanterns gathered round the Glastonbury and other thorns to test the veracity of that year's calendar change. No blooms appeared, confirming the people's suspicion that New Christmas Day, twelve days before the Old, was not the true birthday of Christ—especially since the tree bloomed as usual on 6 January; Quainton villagers were so impressed by the evidence that they refused to attend church on the new feast-day. Acceptance of the calendar change was often slow and even in 1867 one Lancashire man of 77 used the old reckoning as his grandfather and father had done, maintaining stoutly that 'Perliment didn't change t'seeasuns wen they chang'd t'day o't'munth.'[14] Putative progeny of the Glastonbury thorn are widely distributed. A Middlesex example was seen by Elias Ashmole on St Stephen's Day, 1672 'with green leaves, faire buds, and full flowers, all thick and very beautiful', and in 1949 a Herefordshire farmer wrote that many buds of the Orcop thorn opened to full bloom within a few minutes of midnight on Old Christmas Eve.[15] Another descendant blooms in the grounds of the National Cathedral, Washington, DC.[16] Destruction of holy thorns brought swift retribution; an Elizabethan Puritan who injured the Glastonbury tree was blinded in one eye by a flying chip, and a Worcestershire man who felled a tree in the eighteenth century at Redmarley Farm, Acton Beauchamp, broke an arm, then a leg and finally saw his farmhouse damaged by fire, all confidently attributed by local people to a 'judgement'!

THE MUMMERS

Mummers were, and to a small extent still are, part of every country Christmas, appearing at other seasons as pace-eggers, soulcakers and sword-dancers. Their pre-Reformation rituals passed orally from generation to generation. There was no script, but as Walter Rose remembered of Haddenham, Buckinghamshire in the 1870s, the old men knew the words to the last letter and tolerated no variations. The plays include the sword-dance, the wooing and, best known of all, the hero-combat play. All had central themes of antiquity, concerned with primitive vegetation rites symbolising the death and rebirth of summer, played out through presentation, combat, cure and collection.

For one mug of your Christmas ale
Would make us all merry and sing;
And money in our pocket is
A very fine thing . . .

declared the Haddenham mummers. Mumming plays are found as far apart as Newfoundland, Boston and Kentucky, as well as in most English counties.

Principal characters, named at the time of the Crusades, vary little from group to group and include the folk-hero, St George, often transmuted by a long succession of Hanoverian monarchs to King George—'Here comes I, King George, From Old England I did spring . . .', who opposes the Turkish Knight—in country mouths the Turkey Snipe. One is slain, to be miraculously restored by the Doctor with his magic cure-all.

Victorian mummers; at the left stands Father Christmas, masked and wreathed in holly, wassail-bowl in hand. Beside him is the Turkish Knight. St George rides the hobby-horse and to his right the parish beadle announces the play. The Dragon and Doctor with pillbox, complete the group

The Philadelphia mummers, famous for their New Year parade, owe their lavish pageantry more to Swedish than to English settlers, although a surviving fragment of their later eighteenth-century script:

> Here I am, Great Washington,
> On my shoulders I carry a gun . . .

seems to be derived from the English plays:

> In comes I, Beelzebub,
> Over my shoulder I carries my club . . .

Topical characters, heroes and villains of the moment, were added at will—Nelson, Napoleon, the Duke of Cumberland and

> . . . Oliver Cromwell, as you may suppose,
> I conquered many nations with my copper nose.

Minor characters supplied light relief: Old King Cole (with wooden leg), Johnny Jack (with his family of dolls on his back), Beelzebub— took selfconscious places in the space cleared for them.

Village lads the actors might be, well known to everyone in their audience, but a shadow of the old fear and magic remained as they clattered in, disguised, from the frosty lanes, and even in the nineteenth century it was felt unwise to name them, as indeed it still is in Newfoundland.

Costumes were often of brightly-coloured paper strips which hissed and rustled as the mummers played their piece in village inn or lamplit kitchen, wooden swords rattling in the fight. The early nineteenth-century Cornish mummers in the 'Drama of St George' wore white trousers, fluttering ribbons and handkerchiefs and high hats of pasteboard decorated with pieces of looking-glass, beads and paper, with long pieces of peeled rush, and scraps of coloured fabric. William Whittle wrote of strikingly similar costumes in use at St John's, Newfoundland, about 1840, clearly springing from the same origins: the players there wore pasteboard hats covered with costliest wallpaper from which yards of rich ribbon flowed, hiding the players' faces in the time-honoured tradition. On Christmas Eve 1930 the Kentucky play was presented after a lapse of thirty years by 'some men and boys at Gander', for Marie Campbell, who collected the text, which has echoes of the Dorset play.

It was not all laughter. At Great Shefford, where the mummers practised their play with melodeon, tabourine and mouth organ in the skittle alley of the Harrow Inn, one character declared poignantly, reflecting the hard times of the Berkshire labourer:

> Out of nine I got but five,
> Half of they be starved alive.
> We want some money or else some bread,
> Or all the others will soon be dead.

Mumming was a customary part of English village life until 1914. In Newfoundland it survives vigorously, although now confined to the house-visit rather than to the play proper, which died out about 1900–10, and mummers still appear in a few villages such as Overton and Crookham, Hampshire, Marshfield in Gloucestershire and Blewbury, Berkshire.[17]

ST STEPHEN'S DAY AND THE START OF THE YEAR

St Stephen's Day, 26 December, is a time for rural sports. Meets of foxhounds take place everywhere, more for a sociable meeting with friends than for serious hunting; at Winslow, Buckinghamshire where the Whaddon Chase hounds meet by old tradition, the Bell and the George do a roaring trade and church bells ring a merry peal over the market square before hounds move off. Arthur Randell can remember rabbiting with his father in the Norfolk Fens on Boxing or Handbell Day and hearing the frangible Christmas music of the handbell ringers from the village across the fields.

Everywhere the start of the year is marked by church bells. In the Vale of Aylesbury, typifying the English tradition, one tower after another takes up the chain of sound, bell-music floating full and clear over the sleeping farms on the wind, tangling in branches of moonlit elms moving against the winter sky. Sometimes a muffled peal is rung first for the death of the old year, then as the last stroke of midnight dies away, the bells break into a merry open peal to welcome the new year. The bellringers of Over, Cambridgeshire, had their annual supper at the Swan on New Year's Eve, with a hotpot of beer, spirits, eggs, sugar, nutmeg and milk, drunk from a cowhorn nicknamed 'Long Tom'. Many ringers used inscribed pitchers at their 'frolics', and Ixworth ringers, collecting money, carried round their brown-glazed two-gallon pot, dated 1716.

At midnight in Herefordshire the front-door was opened to receive the year and servants rushed to draw the 'cream of the well'—the first water of the new year—for the maid who brought this fortunate gift to her mistress was always rewarded. In the North, just after midnight, comes the important knock of the 'first-footer', a dark man and nominally a stranger, who enters, green sprig in hand, bringing luck to the house. In 1857 Cuthbert Bede saw a Worcestershire farmhouse family rise before dawn to admit the first luck-bringing carol-singer, conducted through the house from front to back.[18]

Ashes are cleared from hearths for a ritual beginning, and silver, bread and coal brought in, symbolising wealth, plenty and warmth. Full cupboards and pockets at the year's start, and a fire blazing through New Year's Eve, ensured prosperity and warmth in coming months. About 1870 a man asked to light his cigar at a cottage near Manchester. 'Nay, Nay, I know better than that,' said the housewife. 'Better than what?' he asked in surprise. 'Better than to give a light out of the house on New Year's Day,' she retorted. The customary philosophy was:

> Take out, then take in, bad luck will begin,
> Take in, then take out, good luck will come about.

William Henderson, warming himself in a Durham farm-kitchen on New Year's Eve about 1860, heard the mistress sternly threaten with instant dismissal any servant who took anything out of the house next day; domestic rubbish was carefully kept indoors until 2 January.

'Apple-gifts', mounted on tripods, trimmed with nuts and yew symbolising sweetness, fertility and immortality, are still offered in the Forest of Dean, Gloucestershire.[19] In Suffolk, luck-giving triangular kitchel cakes and spiced elderberry wine were taken before midnight on New Year's Eve, in St Albans, Hertfordshire 'pope ladies', buns in rough human shape with currants for eyes were eaten, and in Derbyshire a cake made with the first egg laid in the year by the goose.[20] Everywhere, in relics of ancient moon-worship, nine courteous bows to the first new moon of the year and a turning of money in pockets, ensures plenty to come.

TWELFTH DAY AND PLOUGH MONDAY

The quiet pleasures of conversation, stories and carol music were enjoyed on Somerset farms on Twelfth Night and Day, 5 and 6 January, Old Christmas Eve and Day,[21] and in Yorkshire neighbours gathered for mince-pies and the essential wassail-bowl. The holiday was nearly over. On St Distaff's Day, 7 January, women began to spin again after the holiday. The plough was blessed in church on Plough Sunday (as it still is at Exeter, Salisbury, Goathland, Stone,

The Plough Monday procession. The fool dances in animal skins and cow's tail and Bessy carries the collecting bag

Page 103 (above) The yule-log is proclaimed at The Empress Hotel, Victoria, British Columbia; (below) an apple-paring bee in pioneer America about 1859. A girl throws a paring over her shoulder hoping that it will fall in the shape of her lover's initial. From an illustration by Winslow Homer (1836–1910) in *Harper's Weekly, 1859*

Page 104 A bryony root, 16 inches long, presented on 16 May 1916 to Professor Henry Balfour by a labourer of Headington, Oxfordshire, who valued it highly for its magical potency. Now in the Pitt Rivers Museum

Kent and elsewhere, with prayers for a good harvest). On Plough Monday (6 January), ploughing was resumed on the farm, light-heartedly enough for if, when the ploughboy returned from the fields, he could shout 'cock in the pot' before the maid could cry 'cock on the dunghill', the farmer's customary gift of a Shrovetide cockerel would go to the ploughman and not to the maid. Later in the day, young men—plough bullocks, jacks or stots—in white shirts, horse ribbons and rosettes fluttering, bells and brasses on arm and shoulder, roped themselves to a decorated plough for a round of the village along winter-rutted lanes. With sword and morris-dancers and country music of fiddles, pipes or accordion, the procession collected pennies, once for the 'plough light' in the church and later for a frolic. A reluctant donor's doorstep was ploughed up, and the fun, which went on until early this century, is still not quite forgotten.

In the Revesby, Lincolnshire, Plough Monday play, resembling Christmas mumming, the Fool's sons, Pickle Herring, Blue Breeches, Pepper Breeches and Ginger Breeches, lock wooden swords round their father's neck, then with a clatter leap aside and the Fool lies dead:

> Good people all, you see what we have done,
> We have cut down our father like the evening sun.
> And here he lies in all his purple gore,
> And we are afraid he will never dance more.

But at a stamp of Pickle Herring's foot the Fool leaps to his feet delighted at rebirth after death. At Goathland, near Whitby, the Plough Stots, in pink and blue coats, dance with blacksmith-made steel longswords. Characters are the Teamster, with gad and bladder to belabour the Stots, Toms with collecting-boxes, the Gentleman, the Lady, Betty and Auld Isaac, in odd stockings, knee breeches and a black coat with an appliqued red plough and the words 'There he goaz' and 'No man's jig'; and five figures, each beginning with a clash of swords, make up the dance, thought to have come to England with the Norsemen over 1,000 years ago; patterns woven by the dancers culminate in the elevation of the interlaced 'rose' of swords and the ritual 'beheading' of Isaac.[22]

In eastern England the 'Straw Bear', a man completely covered in shining oatstraw, was led round the inns by his keeper to sing and dance, in a ritual, which like many others, died after 1914. One bear, remembered Mrs Kate Mary Edwards, was dressed by his mates during a long, painstaking day's work, then, at the very moment of departure, was 'caught short' and the straw had to be hastily torn off to the ill-concealed fury of the decorators.[23] Plough Monday was the plough-man's day to initiate newcomers to his craft; in Cambridgeshire a boy's nose was rubbed on a horse's vent, or his shoe tapped with a stone, and he might then take his proud place among the teamsmen.

LENT

In country districts Collop Monday precedes Shrove Tuesday and remaining meat was eaten as steaks or collops; on Shrove Tuesday, so-called from the confessions and shriving of the day, eggs were used up in pancakes. As a final indulgence before Lenten austerities, amusements of all kinds occupied the day. In the West of England, Shrove Tuesday is still sometimes Lent-crocking day. 'When the door is opened, the hero, who is perhaps a farmer's boy, with a pair of black eyes sparkling under the tattered brim of his brown milking-hat covered with cow's hair and dirt like the inside of a blackbird's nest, hangs down his head, and, with one corner of his mouth turned up into an irrepressible smile, pronounces the following lines:

> I be come a shrovin,
> Vor a little pankiak,
> A bit o' bread o' your baikin',
> Or a little truckle cheese
> O' your own makin'.
> If you'll gi'me a little, I'll ax no more,
> If you don't gi'me nothin, I'll rottle your door.

If he went unrewarded a rattling broadside of broken earthenware crocks hit the door,[24] and indeed it may still do so in Somerset where the custom survives. Children sing the old Shroving song in the down-land village of East Hendred, Berkshire and are rewarded by the squire, Mr Thomas More Eyston, with a currant bun and ½p.

In Olney, Buckinghamshire, the pancake bell announces the pancake race, run, it is said, since 1450. Housewives in aprons race to church, tossing their pancakes as they go. Since 1950 a parallel race has been run against Liberal, Kansas. The reward is the 'kiss of peace', given in Olney by the verger and in Liberal by the British consul for the area. Winners of both races also receive a prayer-book and a frying-pan from the Liberal Jaycees, and the winning town holds the travelling trophy of an engraved pancake griddle.[25]

Threshing the hen on Shrove Tuesday. The belled carrier of the hen attempts to evade his blindfolded companions who lash out with boughs. The hen will be added to the pancake feast

'Threshing the hen' was a Shrovetide sport and cockfighting and throwing at tethered cocks other cruel pastimes which continued into the nineteenth century, although in Somerset daffodils, called 'Leny-cocks', were substituted. A set of clay cockshies, dated 1791, was found in a Minehead house in 1936, and until about fifty years ago competitors at the Pancake Tuesday Hen Fair, at Wildboarclough, Cheshire, threw long sticks at a bobbin for the prize of a hen. Old Tom Barlow of Oven Farm was so expert a marksman that he declared he never needed to buy a hen.[26] Games of football and hurling mark the day, and at St Columb, Cornwall, the silver hurling ball is dipped into jugs of beer—'silver-beer'—drunk with enjoyment by thirsty players.

MOTHERING SUNDAY

Mothering Sunday, the fourth in Lent, was a holiday for apprentices and daughters in service who visited their mothers carrying a small present of violets, a trinket or simnel cake, a name perhaps derived from the Latin *simila*, fine flour.

> On Mothering Sunday above all other,
> Every child should dine with its mother.

Simnel cakes are still eaten: Shrewsbury, Devizes and Bury, Lancashire (once famous, too, for bragot or spiced ale on Simnel Sunday) are all famous for them. The Shrewsbury cake, filled with rich plumcake mixture, with candied lemon peel, currants, sugar and spices, is tied in a cloth and boiled for several hours, brushed with egg and baked; the crust is as hard as wood and one elderly and short-sighted lady was said to have mistaken her cake for a footstool.

In Hampshire, wafers of thin batter replaced simnel cakes on Wafer-

Shrewsbury simnel cakes

ing Sunday and in Norfolk a special plum-pudding called 'Harvest strengthener'. Another Mid-Lent treat was frumenty. On 29 March 1876, Parson Kilvert gave a bowl of it to old William Pinnock who said that, although as a ploughboy on a farm in Melksham Forest he had been sent to Lacock every Mothering Sunday with a jug of frumenty, he had only tasted it once before in his life. Frumenty was a universal country treat. A correspondent wrote in *Notes and Queries*, 1876, that in his early years on the eastern shore of Maryland it was the standard harvest dish. In Warwickshire a chine of pork was the dish, often followed by fig pudding:

> The lad and lass on Mothering Day,
> Hie home to their mother so dear;
> 'Tis a kiss for she, and a kiss for they,
> A chine of pork and a sprig of bay,
> A song and a dance—but never a tear![27]

Mothering Sunday declined when servants' holidays became general but it was revived to some degree during World War II by American servicemen stationed in England, who were accustomed to celebrating Mother's Day on the second Sunday in May—although Miss Anna Jarvis, who organised the first American celebration in 1906, seems to have been unaware of the older Mid-Lent custom.

EASTER

Palm Sunday passed, with silky grey and yellow willow buds for palm, and Good Friday with hot cross buns, which William Hone regarded, with their cruciate decoration, as the strongest surviving symbol of pre-Reformation England. The joys of Easter, named after the Saxon spring goddess Eostre, whose feast was at the vernal equinox and whose animal was the spring hare, were at hand. Her influence clearly persisted long after Christianity claimed her festival, and the garlands, well-visiting and sunrise observances of Easter are survivals of true vernal rites. Eggs are the Easter symbol, expressing the countryside's new life. Brightly-coloured pace or pasch eggs were begged by children and adults alike. Sometimes dates and mottoes were inscribed with candles upon the warmed eggs, which were then boiled and coloured with tied ribbons, onion skins, herbs and the yellow flowers of gorse and broom, engraved with delicate landscapes, and gilded, polished and preserved in deep ale-glasses in Georgian farmhouse parlours. Coloured eggs were the universal Easter gift; in Somerset they were handed to passengers in all the coaches which stopped at the George Inn, Ilminster. And as late as 1935 the Model Dairy, Caterham, Surrey, sent dyed hens' eggs round to customers on Easter Day.

Derbyshire and Lancashire children carried little baskets lined with moss for oatmeal cakes, money, gingerbread and eggs, all gratefully received. Grown men were not above begging in the nineteenth century, some playing instruments, some dancing, dressed, in one party at least, as Macbeth, a foxhunter, a bishop, Richard III, an Irish umbrella-mender, a quack-doctor and an oyster-catcher. Eggs were played with and rolled (symbolising, it was said, the rolling away of the stone from Christ's tomb) and much mulled ale drunk on a cheerful occasion. North Country children still beg eggs to old rhymes. Since 1877 the greatest egg-rolling ceremony in the world has been enacted on the lawns of the White House, Washington, DC, and egg-and-spoon races have been run in Central Park, New York, for the past thirty Easters.

Jolly-boys or pace-egg players of Far and Near Sawrey in the Lake District, were warmly greeted by Beatrix Potter when they called on her at Castle Cottage and Hill Top Farm. Old Betsy Brownbags, Jolly Jack Tar, Lord Nelson, Old Paddy from Cork and Old Tosspot sang:

> Here's one or two jolly boys all of one mind
> We've come a-pace-egging, I hope you'll prove kind
> I hope you'll prove kind with your eggs and strong beer,
> And we'll come no more nigh you until the next year.[28]

It was believed that the sun danced with joy at the Resurrection on Easter morning. Expeditions were made. 'I was awoke at daylight by Old John, who had come to call me to see the sun dance,' wrote one visitor who was taken up Corndon Tor, Widecombe, Devon in 1876.[29] Sunrise services are another Easter custom and a new tradition began in Southborough, Kent, in 1972, when warmly-clad men and women met for a simple service round a cross of planted daffodils.[30] The first sunrise service of Easter in the United States is held on Cadillac Mountain (the highest point on the Atlantic coast), in the Acadia National Park in the State of Maine, and the last many hours later, on the west coast; and perhaps in a faint recollection of the sun-dancing belief, crowds gather on the shore of Narragansett Bay, Newport, Rhode Island, to see the Easter sunrise. Springs and wells were (and perhaps still are), places of Eastertide pilgrimage. 'What a nasty day for Spanish Waters,' said an Oxfordshire cowman's wife on a cold Palm Sunday about 1935, for then boys and girls of Leafield went into Wychwood Forest with Spanish liquorice to flavour drinks of spring water.

White and gold flowers of spring—Easter lilies or daffodils, Easter roses (double sweet-scented jonquils), pale primroses, none-so-pretty (white or yellow polyanthus), sweet white violets, ivy and catkins, made the Easter garlands for the house, and branches of greenery (never elder or whitethorn), stood before West Country doors.[31] Rich Easter foods, once marking the end of Lent's frugality, are roast lamb and mint sauce, duck, veal or pork with sage, parsley and thyme stuffings (round Ludlow the leg of pork was stuffed with Robin-run-i'-the-hedge, or ground ivy), spinach tarts, custards, clotted cream and from Nottinghamshire to Somerset City, Maryland:

> On Easter Sunday be the Pudding seen
> To which the Tansy lends her sober green.

'Beat seven eggs,' wrote Mrs Rundell in *A New System of Domestic Cookery* (1835) 'yolks and white separately; add a pint of cream, near the same of spinach-juice, and a little tansey-juice gained by pounding in a stone mortar, a quarter of a pound of Naples biscuit, sugar to taste, a glass of white wine, and some nutmeg. Set all in a sauce-pan, just to thicken, over the fire; then put it into a dish, lined with paste, to turn out, and bake it.' The leaves of the pink-spiked bistort, Easter giant, passion dock or Easter ledger make an Easter pudding, especially famous in the Lake District, and often eaten with roast veal. In 1971 a lively tradition was given fresh impetus when the first World

Championship Dock Pudding Eating Contest was held in the Calder Valley, Yorkshire, and fifty competitors came from this valley alone.

Kent enjoyed pudding-pies, flat like pastry-cooks' cheesecakes with a raised crust holding custard and currants. Cherry beer, strong old ale with fermented Kentish cherry juice accompanied this delicacy, offered to coach passengers on the Dover road with the invitation 'Taste the pudding-pies!' Flat spiced Easter cakes are still seen almost everywhere in bakers' shops, descendants of those carried round on Easter Day by parish clerks in the nineteenth century.

To the late nineteenth century women were 'heaved' or 'lifted' by the men on Easter Monday and on the Tuesday the men by the women, in a cheerful ritual said to commemorate the rising from the tomb. Mr Thomas Loggan relished the experience in 1799:

> I was sitting alone last Easter Tuesday, at breakfast, at the Talbot in Shrewsbury, when I was surprised by the entrance of all the female servants of the house, handing in an armchair, lined with white, and decorated with ribbons and favours of different colours. I asked them what they wanted, their answer was they came to *heave* me; it was the custom of the place on that morning, and they hoped I would take a seat in their chair. It was impossible not to comply with a request very modestly made, and to a set of nymphs in their best apparel, and several of them under twenty. I wished to see all the ceremony, and seated myself accordingly. The group then lifted me from the ground, turned the chair about, and I had the felicity of a salute from each.[32]

It was a boisterous day; '. . . we saw a number of females surround a male, whom they mastered, and fairly lifted aloft in the air. It was a merry scene. What humour in the faces of these Lancashire witches! What a hearty laugh! What gratification in their eyes!'[33] Worcestershire farmers' wives actually encouraged the farm-men to lift the women, believing that this would prevent crockery breakages.[34] Rank was no protection; even the parson and squire were lifted if caught. One squire bought himself off with a payment of five shillings.

A correspondent in *Notes and Queries*, September 1883, quoted a letter he had received from an old servant, telling him of lifting. 'When me and Ellen was servants at the Hall, we went in of an Easter Tuesday for to lift the Master. He was that good-natured, was the

A smiling guest is 'heaved' at the Talbot, Shrewsbury, on Easter Tuesday 1799

old Squire; still we was a bit uneasy, and, of course, we knocked at the door first. "Come in," he says. So we come in, and I says, sheepish-like, "If you please, Sir, its Easter Tuesday, and we've coom to lift you." "Aye," he says. "I know what you want, wenches," he says, "but I are too weak. You go to Mrs Smith and ax for five shillings. That's better to lifting o' me." '

APRIL

April, bringing green leaves to the primrose-starred lanes and the beginning of summer, is the month for the cuckoo's plangent call. His arrival never goes unremarked and after his release by the Old Woman from her basket at Heathfield Fair in Sussex on 14 April, First Cuckoo Day, he flies up England carrying warmer days with him. At the bird's first note, even if at noon, nineteenth-century labourers left work, spending the rest of the day at the Cuckoo Ale and turning their money for luck. Devon children always run at the first call, or they will be slow for the year to come, and if Somerset farmers are standing on grass when they hear it, their hay crop is assured. A Cheshire farmer at Antrobus, perturbed by the cuckoo's early arrival in 1944, was relieved to learn that the bird had not been heard within earshot of a field he had ready for oat-sowing for:

> Cuckoo oats and woodcock hay
> Make the farmer run away.

Late oats planted after the cuckoo's arrival will fail, and tardy hay made when woodcock are about, means losses for the farmer.[35]

MAY DAY

On May Day, first day of Celtic summer and prime festival of pastoral England, rooted in pagan fertility rites, whole villages joyfully 'brought in May'—a phrase embracing both the month and sweet-smelling white hawthorn blossom—with maypole dancing and rural sports. Country folk rambled through the green woods on May Eve, blowing cowhorns and calling to each other until dawn, returning home as the sun rose, laden with branches of may blossom to deck their houses and welcome summer. And after the day's merrymaking the sparks from the May fires crackling on the green whirled away on the breeze and a fiddler played again and again for dancing into the night. In the North, May or Beltane fires were lighted well into the eighteenth century.[36]

Puritans in both England and America loathed the day and all it stood for; Philip Stubbes in *The Anatomie of Abuses*, 1583, called the maypole 'This stinking ydol' and sourly denounced the expeditions to the woods, complaining that of perhaps a hundred girls who went 'scarcely the thirde part of them returned home again undefiled.' John Aubrey more temperately regretted the destruction on May Eve of the handsome hawthorns of Woodstock Park, but despite the objections 'bringing home May' persisted long. Even in 1826 the young people of Penzance, Cornwall, went at midnight on May Eve to the farmhouses for junket with sugar, cream and rich country cake. Then with music and laughter, they danced and after gathering hawthorn and making 'May whistles' from twigs, were home again by dawn.

Underlying the pleasure at summer's return was the knowledge that witches were powerful on May Eve and the whole month was witchridden. In Somerset a cross was made with a hazel twig in the hearth ashes and protective marsh-marigold ('John-Georges' in Buckinghamshire) and primrose balls gleamed palely in the spring dusk at house and cowshed door. Parson Kilvert humorously regretted that on May Eve 1870 he had omitted to put birch and rowan over his door at Clyro to keep the witches away.

Maypoles, ubiquitous before the Commonwealth and banned during it, were joyfully restored, often with a crown added, when Charles II returned in 1660. But then Royal Oak Day absorbed the old May Day which gradually faded, although slowly. Washington Irving wrote in 1820 on a visit to England: 'I shall never forget the delight I felt on first seeing a May-pole. It was on the banks of the Dee . . . The mere sight of this May-Pole gave a glow to my feelings, and spread a charm over the country for the rest of the day . . .'.[37] The Victorians, who either misunderstood or ignored the phallic nature of the earlier festivities, revived May Day in expurgated form, but, wrote a disappointed visitor: 'It lacked the healthy rusticity which I had anticipated from the hearty enjoyment of lusty farm labourers and their sweethearts in the old-fashioned May-day dance.'[38] Maypoles are still a part of life in some villages. Barwick-in-Elmet maypole, in the custody of elected polemen, is lowered every third year for repairs and new garlands, and Lanreath villagers set a living tree on their green as a maypole. Since maypoles were of a straight-growing ash, pine or larch, they were seldom wasted; when disused they became house-beams or ladders. The Chalgrove, Oxfordshire, maypole, engraved with a large M, could, about 1883, be seen as a rafter in a barn.[39]

The May Queen, prettiest girl in the village, sat in a leafy arbour near the maypole and Jack-in-the-Green, alias the May King, or Green Man, wreathed in oak and hawthorn leaves with only face exposed, acted death, but magically sprang to life to dance with her. Mr Ernest Shepard, the artist, remembers that as a child in St John's Wood, London, in the 1880s, he was frightened by a cavorting Jack-in-the-Green group with a Bessy-like figure catching donated coins in her parasol,[40] and in 1871 Parson Kilvert saw two women carrying a Jack-in-the-Green in Hereford. The Green Man, leaves growing from his mouth, survives on inn-signs and in hundreds of vigorous church carvings, the very embodiment of leafy May.

At Randwick, Gloucestershire, the people enjoyed May Day cheeses: 'Three large cheeses (Gloucester of course), decked with the gayest flowers of this lovely season, are placed on litters, equally adorned with flowers, and boughs of trees waving at the corners. They are thus borne through the village, accompanied by a joyous throng, shouting and huzzaaing with all their might and main, and

Children with cowhorns parading the May garlands at King's Lynn, Norfolk, about 1820. A May-doll rests among flowers and festoons of blown birds' eggs toss within

usually accompanied by a little band of music.' The cheeses were then bowled three times round the church before distribution.[41] Until the last century Temple Sowerby, Westmorland, held a story-telling contest on the village green on May Day. The greatest liar won; the first prize was a grindstone, the second a razor hone and smaller prizes marked lesser liars. Once the Bishop of Carlisle was passing and, seeing the crowd, descended majestically from his carriage to give a great lecture on the evils of lying, ending ' "For my part I never told a lie in my life . . ." This was immediately reported to the judges, upon which, without any dissent, the hone was awarded to his lordship as most deserving of it; and, as is reported, it was actually thrown into his carriage.' Tall-story competitions were also held in inns, and an iron medal, $1\frac{1}{4}$ inches in diameter, inscribed 'The Noted Liar', found in the garden of the Pike and Eel, Chesterton, Cambridgeshire, in 1964, was perhaps a prize in such a contest.[42]

Any Suffolk servant bringing her mistress a branch of creamy hawthorn blossom on May morning, was rewarded with a dish of cream for breakfast. But this ritual breaking of the taboo against hawthorn in the house died a natural death with the calendar changes of 1752, for blossom was then rarely in bloom so early in the month.

In 1861 one man who found a party of four singers with flute and clarinet on his lawn at Swinton, Yorkshire, was told the words of two May songs sung there: the 'Old May Song'—'All in This Pleasant Evening', and the 'New May Song'—'Come Listen Awhile':

> Come listen awhile unto what we shall say,
> Concerning the season, the month we call May;
> For the flowers they are springing, and the birds they do sing,
> And the baziers are sweet in the morning of May . . .[43]

Oxfordshire children still recite such rhymes as:

> Good morning, missus and master,
> I wish you a happy day,
> Please to smell my garland
> Because it's the first of May.

As they did when Flora Thompson wrote of children about 1880 dressed as king and queen, lord and lady, and maids of honour, carry-

In this print of about 1860 small girls show their May garlands to ladies of the 'big house'

ing willow wands topped with the flamboyant yellow crown imperial and garlands of leaves, wallflowers, bluebells, yellow cowslips from the mowing grass, pink and white ladysmocks, cuckoo-flowers or milkmaids, red flowering-currant, daisies and sweet briar, fixed to a wooden framework, with a doll—'the lady'—within. Muslin draped over the garland was removed only after a donation, and the procession moved off, to walk many miles round farms, cottages, rectory and 'big house'.[44] In 1796 Anne Hughes gave her young visitors May-day cakes—of meat, apple, onion and lemon thyme, rosemary and black sugar, in a pastry case.

In some counties May Day is still Garland Day. 'When we arrived here in 1960,' writes Mrs Baker from Weston Turville, Buckinghamshire, 'the children still came round with garlands . . . the tiny ones with

A Northamptonshire May garland

Morris-dancers on the painted glass window, Betley, Staffordshire.
(1) Robin Hood alias the May King; (2) Maid Marian in golden crown
holds a summer pink; (3) Friar Tuck; (5) Hobby-horse with ladle for
donations; (9) the piper with tabor, and (12) the fool with bauble, a
coxcomb hood and ass's ears. The other figures are morris-dancers

bunches of flowers and the older ones with arrangements on a tray. These, cushion-like, more like funeral emblems, had a cross as a focal point and were mostly of garden flowers—narcissi, wallflowers and polyanthus and a little early may from the field hedges.' As a group, the children recited a verse ending 'So please remember the garland...' exactly as they had said to John Brand on May Day 1791, 'Pray, Sir, remember the garland.'

An artist's impression of the same dancers on the green

Robin Hood and May games, with dancing and sports such as archery and cudgel play, mingled at an early date and the perennial woodland hero assumed the mantle of the older May King. Maid Marian as May Queen, Friar Tuck, Little John, the hobby-horse and fool, moved among the morris-dancers on the green, jingling their ancient figures on a bright summer morning. The painted-glass window at Betley, Staffordshire, said to date from the reign of Henry VIII, showed these characters and a streaming maypole pennant inscribed 'A Mery May'.

Morris-dancers appeared at other seasons also. Mr J. R. Prior saw a group of eight young men at Clerkenwell in June 1826, ribbons on hat and arm and latten bells at knee. Six danced while the seventh, the 'arch dark-featured Lubin Brown' whose 'ear was alive to Doric melody', played the pipe and tabor and the leader held the collecting-box. The haunting tune 'the little rural-noted pipe played to the gentle pulsations of the tabor, is called

> Moll in the wad and I fell out,
> And what d'ye think it was about?'

—one of Charles Dibdin's street songs. They had come from a Hertfordshire village, they said, and would stay in London for a week or two before dividing up the contents of the box and going home to start mowing and hay-harvest. It was their third year of pilgrimage to London and they had never once disputed on the road.[45] Today the dancing season usually begins about May Day, groups perform in many villages and one team at Bampton claims an unbroken history of five hundred years.

AFTER MAY DAY: WHITSUN

May Day merriment spilled over into the month. The Furry Dance still takes place at Helston, Cornwall, on 8 May, and about 1825 a visitor to the little market town of Buckingham on the first Sunday in May found the bells 'ringing the old bailiff out'. 'As the musicians . . . came nearer with the accumulating procession, I with difficulty learned the theme of their endeavours to be Weber's "Hark! Follow!" I never heard anything to surpass this murder of melody . . .' A flower-decorated procession of children and dancers followed, then the bailiff himself—'a sir John Falstaff-like sort of person'—and the burgesses in robes, with nosegays, all in their Sunday best.[46]

Whitsun was the season for walks and feasts of village friendly societies which were, in some measure, the final manifestation of the sociability of the old village wake. When Arthur Beckett attended a Sussex club walk about 1908 he found members in their best, with insignia of red, blue and green sashes and silver stars, clattering with hobnailed boots into a church service. While the band played, dinner was served in a tent on the green, with joints of cold beef, legs of South Down mutton, ham, meat pies, pressed beef, pickled onions and salads. Jellies, custards, fruit tarts and cheese and plenty of beer followed, with speeches and singing. Participants were mostly small farmers and tradesmen, many with such bouquet-like buttonholes of summer flowers that they could scarcely turn their heads.[47]

In the nineteenth century at Lytchett Matravers, Dorset, club members in Sunday smocks, gay neckerchiefs and garlands, paraded on Trinity Monday with painted wooden club signs. The best garland received a prize, church followed and the procession and band (which existed principally for the club walk) went round to give the farmers a tune, to collect donations and to enjoy cider brought out in great jugs. The day ended with dinner at Higher Lytchett inn and dancing far into the night. 'Almost like a fair,' said villagers with satisfaction.

Walks continue in a few villages, or only ceased with World War II and the development of social services which diminished the role of friendly societies. At Fownhope, Herefordshire, the Heart of Oak Friendly Society still walks about 29 May, with staves decorated with wooden oak-apples, and at East Hagbourne, Berkshire, guelder roses decorating the president's chair at the club dinner on Feast Day in Manor Farm barn, are 'club bunches'.

As for Whitsun food, all true Sussex people ate roast veal and goose-berry pudding and great the indignation if the gooseberries were not ripe in time,[48] and in Worcestershire and Shropshire, farmers gave all the milk of their cows to neighbours who cared to call for it on Whit-Sunday morning.

ROYAL OAK DAY: 29 MAY

When Charles II claimed his throne in 1660, England joyfully insti-
tuted a new holiday, 29 May, Royal Oak or Oakapple Day, named
after the tree in which the the king had hidden so romantically after
Worcester Fight in 1651, and the date both of his birthday and of his
public re-entry into London. The oak leaf was its happy symbol.
Hampshire labourers rose early to gather oak sprigs for hats and door
knockers and after breakfast begged for beer, calling rudely if refused:

> Shig-shag, penny a rag,
> Bang his head in Cromwell's bag,
> All up in a bundle!

Alternative names for the day were Shick-Shack or Shig-Shag. Those
not wearing oakleaves were taunted, nettled or pinched; indeed in
many villages children not wearing emblems are still in danger.
Keepers were indulgent to trespassers in the woods on Oakapple Day
and in Dorset, where gilded leaves were correct, country stationers
laid in special supplies of gold leaf.[49] Carters dressed their horses'
bridles with oakleaves and in many villages, oak boughs were tied to
church towers while the bells pealed merrily.

In the Devon market town of Tiverton in the early nineteenth
century, young men in seventeenth-century dress with swords, paraded
with 'Oliver Cromwell', face blackened and held firmly on a strong
cord. The prisoner, chosen for his sporting disposition, obligingly
capered and pranced while the townspeople threw dirt at him, but
any saucy small boy he caught was smeared with soot to the delight
of the crowd. Men followed carrying a small child within a litter of
oak boughs, symbolising the pleasure felt at the fresh beginning of the
king's return.

MIDSUMMER

The summer solstice, about 21 June, a time for magic and divination,
lighted by aestival fires to honour and strengthen the sun, was transferred by the early church to the feast of St John the Baptist on 24 June.

Then fires of dry midsummer wood, circled by dancers moving ever sunwise, blazed and crackled through the short night, their smoke drifting over uneasy cattle penned nearby, wreathed in St John's wort against the witches powerful at the solstice. Farm stock was driven through the dying embers and a Somerset farmer's daughter remembered at Holford in 1915 that an old farmer always passed a lighted branch over and under all their cows and horses at Midsummer, and singed the foals and calves in an ancient ritual of protection, which he refused to explain.[50] Midsummer fires gleamed on northern hills until the mid-nineteenth century and still burn in Cornwall, where their ashes are charms. In Somerset at Midsummer, even in this century, flowers were placed for luck on the largest stone on the farm, in a remnant of a Celtic floral sacrifice.

'I remember once,' wrote William Coles in *Adam in Eden*, 1657, of Midsummer, 'as I rid through Little Brickhill in Buckinghamshire . . . every signe-post in the towne almost, was bedeckt with green birch.' Other protective plants on this witch-ridden night were fennel, orpine, vervain, trefoil (suggesting the Trinity) and rue. Over the cowshed door hung a wreath of sulphur-yellow St John's wort, leaves red-flecked, it was said, with the blood of the martyred saint. Within the last fifty years rowan was tied with red thread to cows' tails on Mid-summer Night and prudent travellers tucked rowan sprigs into their horses' bridles. Fernseed, almost invisible, and by the same token giving the gift of invisibility to its possessor, was collected on St John's Eve, but the work was dangerous to the gatherer. The plant must never be directly touched but rather bent with a forked hazel stick over a pewter plate (associated with the communion paten); there were great difficulties and gatherers who thought they had done well found empty pockets when they arrived home. Fernseed was collected into the nineteenth century in eastern North America and even in 1867 it was still infallibly held in Lancashire that fernseed collected on the family Bible would give the desired gift of invisibility. Lucky hands or St John's hands were made from the rootstock of the male fern, trimmed to a likeness of thumb and fingers, smoked in Midsummer fires and hung for long-lasting protection in house and barton.

LAMMASTIDE AND THE FAIRS

At Lammas, 1 August, until the enclosures, stock was put to pasture on the hay-meadows, which then remained common until spring. William Plastow, a farm labourer of Haddenham, born in 1839, seven years after the enclosures were completed there, remembered hearing that the common grazing of the village had lain in big meadows by the stream to Scotsgrove Mill, and along the river Thame to Notley Abbey. Hay was made by the freeholders, and the meadows opened for grazing on Lammas Day. The calamitous date in the history of this Buckinghamshire village—1832—when the ancient privilege was extinguished, bringing wealth to some but poverty to more, was carved in wry remembrance on a beam in the barn at Hewdon Farm.[51]

Lammas was the season of first fruits, and derived from the old English *hláfmaesse*, loaf-mass, for a ritual loaf was made from the first new wheat. A shadow of the old ways survives at Richmond, Yorkshire, where the first farmer to bring a sample of threshed Lammas wheat to the mayor as clerk of the market, on an arranged day usually in September, receives a bottle of wine.

Autumn months, when harvesting was over and the farm had a few quiet weeks before its round began again, was the time for the business and pleasure of fairs. Old villagers in Lambourn, among the Berkshire Downs, remember the clamour of the sheep fair on 4 December, Old St Clement's Day, when flocks of sheep with shepherds and barking dogs, passed up and down the village street all day, stalls sold sweets and toys, and after they had finished business farmers bought Clementy cakes, with butter, currants, peel, sugar and spices, baked in Wantage until about 1895, and brought up the hill by cart. Fairs were notable events in the rural mind. About 1860 a young immigrant to the United States, asked his age, replied 'Nineteen come last Lambourn Fair.' At Weyhill sheep fair on Old Michaelmas Day, over £250,000 would change hands and gold sovereigns were carried home in leathern bags by satisfied farmers wearing their best blue coats with brass buttons, for this important occasion.

Aylesbury had its Fig Fair, Tavistock a Michaelmas Goose Fair,

Stow-on-the-Wold still has flourishing horse fairs in May and October and Findon a Lamb Fair in July. Woodbury Hill, keenly anticipated by Dorset folk, had five fairs to suit all tastes and pockets; Wholesale, Gentlefolks', Allfolks', Sheepfair and Pack-and-Penny, when remaining goods were sold cheaply on the last day.

For country servants seeking new jobs, however, the hiring fair, often at Martinmas or Michaelmas, was a critical day of the year, for a 'good place' was the ambition of all. A humorous duologue well liked at early nineteenth-century harvest home feasts in Warwickshire described the scene:

> Farmer: Come all you lads that be here for service,
> Come here, you jolly dogs:
> Who will help me with my harvest,
> Milk my cows and feed my hogs?
>
> Yonder stands as likely a fellow,
> As e'er trod in leathern shoe,
> Canst thou plough, and canst thou harrow?
> Servant: O yes, master! and I can milk too!
>
> Farmer: Here's five pounds in standing wages,
> Daily well thou shalt be fed,
> With good cabbage, beef and bacon,
> Butter-milk, and oaten bread.
>
> Here's a shilling, take it yarnisht,
> And a Thursday thou must come;
> For my servants do all leave me,
> And my work it must be done.[52]

The hiring contract, even in the 1930s, was sealed with the earnest or yarnisht shilling.

At hiring fairs often called 'mop' fairs, those seeking work wore emblems of their callings; a maid carried a mop, '*A carter* exhibits a piece of whip-cord tied to his hat; a *cowherd* has a lock of cow-hair in his; and *the dairy-maid* has the same descriptive mark attached to her breast.'[53] 'Runaway mops' held a week or two later allowed servants and employers dissatisfied with their bargains to try again. They stood waiting, under the blue autumn skies, pungent scents of apples, cows and gingerbread about them, for what fate held in store. All were agreed on the seriousness of the first part of the day's proceedings; those thinking of new jobs in Lincolnshire noticed the direction in which the first lamb of the year was seen lying, for thence lay new

A Warwickshire hiring-fair about 1825. A labourer in his best round-frock wears a flower in his hat and a maidservant her white apron

work and Norfolk servants leaving for the fair had a shoe thrown after them for luck. Gaiety stepped in as soon as hiring was completed and the girls picked sweethearts. In Chester as the fair closed, hundreds of farm servants in their best, with a year's wages jingling in their pockets, thronged the streets, buying new clothes, ribbons and trinkets, and benefitting tavernkeepers and shopkeepers.

At Kendal hiring fair in 1846, 'the girls were all ages, from thirteen to thirty, looking remarkably healthy, and fully maintaining the compliment of the "bonny lasses of Westmoreland"..."What do you ask" said a farmer to a smart-looking girl. "Five pound." "Ah! That's above my cut," and after some further enquiries as to where she had lived, he added, "That's o'er fine a place for me." Another, haggling a long time with a young woman, presented a shilling to her, as cattle-dealers do to each other, consenting to give what she asked, but wanting "five shillings out". "Stick up tull him," replied a motherly old woman who stood near; and shortly after, the bargain was struck for the whole amount, by the shilling being placed in her hand...' The girls showed great freedom in asking the applicants questions:—'Where is your house? How many kye do you keep? What is there to do?' One farmer thought to curry favour by answering 'Oh, we have nothing to do.' 'Then I'll not hire with you,' was the brisk reply.[54] Mrs Baker writes of her mother's girlhood in Canterbury, Kent, about 1868:

> She told me how she always enjoyed going to the Michaelmas Hiring Fair, where she liked to listen to the farmers re-engaging their labourers for another spell of work. They would walk up to particular workers who had satisfied them during past service and say, 'Pawk agin, er'ow?' Her father explained that this was 'Pork again or how?', ie 'Will you have pork again with me, or what will you do?'[55]

Gradually employment exchanges developed; the number of agricultural workers declined with farm mechanisation and people drifted from the land during the Depression. Farm workers became content to stay in the same place for longer periods. The old pattern began to change for good between 1900 and 1914 and hiring fairs as such diminished although many continue today on their traditional dates, as pleasure fairs only.

HALLOWE'EN, ALL SOULS' AND OTHER NOVEMBER FESTIVALS; THE END OF THE YEAR

The last night of October, Old Year's Night in the Celtic calendar, a night of witches and fires, was transmuted by the Church into the vigil of All Saints' or Hallowe'en, still celebrated in the North of England with disguises, divination and candlelit turnip-lanterns, jumping for treacled scones and ducking for apples. Until at least 1890 Cornish greengrocers laid in stocks of fine Allan apples, the traditional gift for children at All Hallows. Precautions must be taken on this night of enchantment. Journeys must be finished before sunset, and a piece of bread crossed with salt (holy bread with witch-repellent salt) was a safe pocketful for the traveller. A rowan cross in hand or on bridle was another safeguarding device, remembered and perhaps observed in Somerset this century. A lighted candle left burning all

Ducking for apples at Hallowe'en

night in the stable kept evil from farm stock, and villagers advised each other never to leave a door ajar or an unwelcome supernatural visitor might enter and remain with the household for life. Hallowe'en customs took firm hold in North America, where pumpkins replace turnip-lanterns and crowds of begging children often disguised as witches make their round calling 'trick or treat'. A disobliging householder may find his windows soaped or garbage cans overturned.

In Lancashire, 'lating' or 'lighting the witches' was an important

Hallowe'en rite. One woman remembered lating on Longridge Fell in 1818 with a party of thirty, carrying candles about the hills from eleven until midnight. If the candles burned steadily the carriers were safe for a season, but if the witches blew them out, the omen was bad indeed. 'Teanlas' or 'tinley' fires glowed on northern hills on All Souls' Eve, 1 November, symbolising the ascent to heaven of souls in purgatory and only the enclosures (when bushes were grubbed up) put an end to the small 'tindles', lighted in the furze of Derbyshire commons. In one Lancashire field near Poulton, called Purgatory by the old folk, men stood in a circle to throw forkfuls of burning straw high in the air on the night breeze, and all present fell to their knees praying for the souls of the departed. More prosaically, some farmers maintained that the procedure was useful against the weed darnel.

High heaps of flat spiced 'soulcakes' stood ready for all who called on 2 November, All Souls' Day, and they were begged for by grown men in the last century. Still sung by Cheshire and Shropshire children, asking for small treats, is:

> Soul! Soul! for a soul cake,
> I pray, good missis, a soul cake,
> An apple, or pear, a plum or a cherry,
> Any good thing to make us merry...

and in Comberbach, Cheshire, the soulcakers' play is performed by a mummer-like group with the Hodening or Wild Horse.

Some Hallowmass fires were transferred to Guy Fawkes Day, 5 November, and still blaze in garden and on green. At Hartley Wintney, Hampshire, villagers carrying flaming torches assemble at four points round the village to cross the green, and at a signal to toss two hundred brands on to the great bonfire. Even three days later its ashes are hot enough to roast chestnuts.[56]

A cluster of November saints cheered the dark days of the year's end. The feast of St Clement on 23 November (first day of winter Old Style) and St Catherine on 25 November were, through their proximity, linked in the beggars' song:

> Cattern' and Clemen', be here, be here,
> Some of your apples and some of your beer...

St Clement was the patron saint of the jovial tribe of blacksmiths, and on his day they fired gunpowder on their anvils. At the Wealden village of Burwash, as late as about 1865, 'Old Clem' with wig, beard and pipe, stood over the tavern door while the smiths feasted within. St Catherine was the saint of lacemakers and on Cattern Day until about 1890 when the lace trade declined, children of the Midland laceschools chose a queen and in white dresses walked the winter villages for money and cakes. As late as 1900 'wiggs', round spongy buns of fine flour with caraway seeds, were eaten at Wendover, Buckinghamshire at Catterntide, with a drink of warm beer, rum and eggs. Catherine wheels spun and sparkled for the saint, and in the evening the girls drew up their skirts to play the old country game of leap-candle, jumping back and forth for luck over a lighted lace-maker's candle set upon the floor, to the rhyme:

> The tailor of Bister, he has but one eye,
> He cannot cut a pair of green galagaskins,
> If he were to die.[57]

Somerset farmers still eat a spoke of Cattern pie, shaped like a Catherine wheel, with a filling of mincemeat, honey and crumbs, to bring luck and a safe winter to the farm.[58]

St Thomas's Day, 21 December, marking the winter solstice ('St Thomas Gray, St Thomas Gray, Longest night and shortest day') was, like Shrove Tuesday, a day for 'barring out' the schoolmaster from the village-school and this fun over, Christmas was at hand again and the ring of the year complete.

5

From Cradle to Grave

The cycle of life—birth, marriage and death—has special meaning for country people, accustomed as they are to its seasonal reflection in garden, hedgerow and farm. Divination of matters so rich in chance has always been inviting, and until Victorian inhibition sapped their vitality, christenings, weddings and funerals were celebrated with all the boisterousness of bedding the bride, kimbly cake and funeral feast. The old rural community readily comprehended a birth as a valuable addition to the work-force, a marriage as a new working partnership and a death as the loss of ancient skills and wisdom.

Country life fosters acceptance of life's lottery. An old gardener of Hartley Wintney, still working at eighty, came in for dinner one day and enjoyed a great plate of his favourite clove and apple pie. He asked for a second helping, his daughter turned aside to cut it for him and in that moment he died, spoon still in hand. Later she said reflectively; 'Well, I suppose his time was up, but I'm glad he had his pie before he went.'[1] The acceptance is free from morbidity. 'We be but leaves', the simple epitaph on a Dartmoor tombstone, tells the story.

THE CRADLE

The sex of an unborn child was even more keenly a matter for speculation in the past when a boy was often greatly preferred. In Denbighshire about 1850, an old woman used this charm. Dining with the servants on a mutton shoulder she scorched the bone at the fire, pushing her thumbs through the thin part and stringing the bone up over the back door, giving the servants instructions to watch closely for the sex of the first caller to enter the doorway the following morning. To the servants' great delight, and contrary to the usual occurrence, the first caller was a man, portending the birth of a boy, which came about a few weeks later. The old woman's reputation as a seer was made.

May was an ill-omened month for birth—'A May baby's sickly— you may try, but you'll never rear it,' was a general verdict. Sunday was the luckiest day of the week, Christmas Day the luckiest of the year and Childermas, 28 December, by far the least auspicious day for birth. The earlier in the day the child was born the better—'the later the hour the shorter the life'—and birth during the moon's increase meant the child would grow quickly. 'The moon's change brings babies on', is another belief. A 'chime child' born between midnight on Friday and cockcrow on Saturday (although the phrase can also mean birth at four, eight or twelve, or at three, six, nine or twelve), is favoured with second sight. Ruth Tongue, the Somerset folklorist, is a chime child who saw her first ghost at Taunton Castle, Somerset, when a small girl. She remembers his black periwig, red sash and unhappy face, and believes him to have been a Monmouth rebel sentenced by Judge Jeffreys in 1685.

When the midwife arrived she unlocked doors and loosened all knots, analogous to an easy birth. The baby was first bathed before a protective ashwood fire in Devon, and its head washed in rum, for luck, in Cumberland. Its first drink 'to drive Satan away' was cinder tea, water in which a coal had been dropped, or sap from the ash tree, against witchcraft. In Shropshire its first food was butter and sugar, signifying richness to come. The belief that in order 'to rise in the world' the child must go up before it went down was widespread. If the birth took place in a bedroom and no stairs were available, the nurse holding the infant, stepped up on to a chair or box. It was held that no woman should leave her home before churching (the service of thanks for safe delivery in days of greater obstetrical dangers), since she would have no legal redress for any insult offered her before the ceremony. Many of these beliefs survive and even in 1941 the

Rev Peter B. C. Binnell of Holland Fen, Lincolnshire, wrote that he had been asked to 'set Mrs —— at liberty' by churching her.[2]

There was a widespread prejudice against weighing the newlyborn, perhaps linked with the country dislike of revealing personal data lest they be used in witchcraft. Taboos ruled the management of babies: the child must not see itself in a mirror, have right hand washed, or hair or nails cut, before weaning. Most mothers felt happier when christening was over (it is still widely sought, even by non-believers), and sanctified font-water was prized for cures and witch-craft. In the mid-nineteenth century the old monthly nurse of Church-down, Gloucestershire, rinsed the infant's mouth with font-water left after christening, assuring the vicar that this would prevent toothache. At least eleven fonts in Somerset alone have locked covers to prevent sacrilegious theft of the water, which might also be protected by the addition of salt.[3] A new baby would be offered the customary gifts of an egg, silver and salt, typifying fertility, wealth and protection from enchantment; gifts which, Major Fairfax-Blakeborough writes (1972), are still presented round Westerdale.

A real fear for mothers in remote districts as late as the last century was that fairies might steal their babies and leave cross fairy-children in their place. Wise Devon mothers pinned their babies' shawls to dresses or pillows to thwart attempted theft; and in an echo of the hatching lore of the poultry yard, thirteen or more primroses were laid, a safe handful, under a Somerset baby's cradle. In the early eighteenth century George Waldron was shown a supposed changeling in the Isle of Man, a beautiful child who although five years old could not walk or stand and never spoke or cried, although if anyone called him a 'fairy-elf' he fixed his frowning gaze on the speaker. Curious neighbours peering in at the cottage window would see him laughing with delight and concluded that he was not alone, for he would always be washed, with hair combed, when his mother returned from her work.[4]

Until about 1900 it was customary in many counties for a 'groaning' or 'sickening' cake, cheese and ale, to be provided for nurse and neighbours immediately after the birth, a celebration called in Shrop-shire the 'merry meal'. In Northumberland the cheese was distributed to all houses, to males if the baby were a boy, and to females if a girl. Emigrants carried the custom far and wide, and it was known in Newfoundland as late as 1890.[5]

Bachelors in eighteenth-century Eastbourne, Sussex, made an occasion called 'sops and ale' of births among wives of wealthy farmers or tradesmen. The senior bachelor of the village, named steward, was given twelve wooden knives and forks, trenchers and other utensils and announced the feast in church, wand of office in hand. The company divided itself among tables in the new father's house; at the top table, with fine silver and china, sat the 'benchers', happy fathers of twins; at the second table, with plainer appointments, sat fathers of one or more children, and at the third table, without tablecloth, sat the married but childless and the old bachelors, with the wooden furnishings provided by the steward. The party was merry indeed with 'proper toasts . . . appropriate for the occasion'.

A Devon squire told in *The Western Morning News*, 4 January 1883, of another custom. 'I was driving the other day, when on passing a market trap, I suddenly had a cake thrust into my hand, amidst shouts of "The Squire has get 'en". I said, "Really I am much obliged, but I do not want it." "Oh, but you must have it; it is the christening cake," was the rejoinder, shouted out by the now passing occupants of the trap. After they had driven on, I asked my coachman (who has lived in the parish a full forty years), whether he could explain the matter; and he told me that, "the cake was given to the first person that was met by a christening party on the way to church". I accordingly gave the cake to him, as he was on the box, and therefore was clearly entitled to it. He was delighted; he said, "I've heard tell of the custom all my life, but this is the first time I have ever met with it."' In poorer families the presentation of bread and cheese was quite correct.

When Kenneth Grahame, the writer, stood godfather at Fowey, Cornwall, in 1907 to the youngest son of his American friends, Mr and Mrs Austin Purves of Philadelphia, the old christening cake custom—called 'kimbly' in Cornwall—was observed[6] and it seems to have continued at least as late as 1932. The recipient of the gift must usually give three things back to the infant with his good wishes, and one gentleman unexpectedly accosted rose inventively to the occasion with a shilling, a halfpenny and a pinch of snuff.

LOVE AND MARRIAGE

St Valentine's Day, 14 February, festival of lovers and in country lore the day upon which birds choose their mates, was once a serious occasion upon which future marriages might turn. Valentines were chosen, for a girl either the first man she met in the morning, or one drawn by lot. Cards were sent:

> The rose is red, the violet blue,
> Honey is sweet and so are you,

was a rhyme to delight rustic tastes.

The divination of prospects of love and marriage was constantly intriguing, and hundreds of rituals faithfully performed in cottage bedroom or farmhouse kitchen helped to reveal the future. Girls still throw an apple paring over their shoulders in the hope that it may fall in the shape of their lovers' initials.

> I pare this pippin round and round again,
> My shepherd's name to flourish on the plain.
> I fling th'unbroken paring o'er my head,
> Upon the grass a perfect L is read,

wrote John Gay in *The Shepherd's Week*. The procedure enlivened the apple-paring 'bees' of pioneer North America.

A divination practised within living memory required good courage for, throwing hempseed over her shoulder, a girl walked through garden or churchyard on Midsummer Eve, saying:

> Hempseed I set, hempseed I sow,
> The man that is my true love,
> Come after me and mow,

and behind her, mowing or raking into a winding-sheet, would appear the phantom of her future husband. From her Herefordshire farmhouse window on 22 June 1796, Anne Hughes watched her maid Sarah sowing hemp in the stable yard as the clock struck twelve, inviting the carter's lad, with whom she was walking out, to appear. Anne remembered that she too had done this before she married her husband John, although she ruefully admitted that since he had gone nowhere near the place of sowing, she felt little confidence in the charm's efficacy.

Nuts named for lovers were set upon the hearthstone on St Mark's Eve to the rhyme:
> If you love me pop and fly
> If not lie there silently

Shoes were arranged carefully by bedsides on Midsummer Eve to the rhyme:
> Hoping this night my true love to see
> I place my shoes in the form of a T,

and in Maryland more elaborately to:
> Point your shoes towards the street,
> Tie your garters around your feet;
> Put your stockings under your head
> And you'll dream of the one you're going to wed.

The succulent green *sedum telephium*, orpine, midsummer-men or lifelong—so-named because it remained green long after plucking—was stuck in the doorpost on Midsummer Eve: if by next morning it had inclined to the right the lover was faithful, but if to the left no wise girl should trust him. The traditional role of this plant was confirmed by the finding at Cawood, Yorkshire, in 1801, of a fifteenth-century ring inscribed *Ma fiancée velt* and two midsummer-men joined by a lovers' knot. And finally in a West Country ritual favouring shy suitors, a girl would pick a rose on Midsummer Day and put it away in white paper; it would not fade, and if she wore it to church on Christmas Day her lover would reveal himself in silence by taking it from her.

'Bundling' was a courtship practice found especially in Wales and along the Welsh border and despite appearances was said to be of complete propriety. The couple 'bundled' or slept together in the same bed, fully dressed, separated by a board laid down the bed's middle. The custom was carried to New England and Pennsylvania and on to Canada by the United Empire Loyalists and survived until the mid-nineteenth century. Prudent mothers gave daughters approaching the bundling age a 'courting-stocking' completely covering the girl's body from the waist downwards, with room for both legs within it; such stockings, in use in Wales until the late nineteenth century, were often heirlooms. The practice was fully accepted; when the vicar of Little Ouse, Cambridgeshire, called on a family to reprove the eldest son for bundling, he was told: 'But vicar, you wouldn't buy a horse without getting astride it to see how it trotted.'[7]

The choice of wedding day is still significant. May is generally avoided: 'Marry in May, rue for aye'. The Rev Alfred Gatty wrote from Ecclesfield, Yorkshire, on 29 April 1850, that a colonial bishop and an archdeacon were both taking part in weddings at his church on that day, and both had been asked to perform the ceremonies not later than 30 April, for neither bride would consent to be married in May. Lent was just as bad—'Marry in Lent, live to repent' was the discouraging pronouncement, and the day of the week is portentous:

> Monday for wealth, Tuesday for health,
> Wednesday best day of all,

Thursday for losses, Friday for crosses,
And Saturday no luck at all.

Traditions ruled the day. Should the farmer's younger son or daughter marry before the elder, the latter must dance barefoot in the hogtrough wearing green stockings, to avert the ill-luck of this happening. When a Sussex miller's son was married the millsweeps were locked in the cross position called 'miller's glory' to bring luck to the union. The Rev Cuthbert Bede reported in *Notes and Queries*, 1857, that after a Worcestershire village wedding he found the great bell was set moving to 'fore-tell' the number of children the couple might have. He heard it toll nine times and wrote: 'The bride and bridegroom know, therefore, what to expect, and can make the needful preparations for the advent of their tuneful nine.' And at Shropshire village weddings until at least 1840 'all the silver spoons, tankards,

A Tudor walking-wedding at Hampton Lucy, Warwickshire

watches, and ornaments of the neighbouring farmers were fastened on white cloths drawn over hoops, so as to make a kind of trophy on each side of the church gate . . .'[8]

Into the nineteenth century, country bridal parties walked to church along a path strewn with flowers, rushes and wheat. In Guernsey the wild marsh-iris was a favourite strewing flower, and rosemary, marigolds and broom were commonly seen. Many myrtle bushes with shining leaves and white flowers at cottage doors, owe their existence to the old country usage of planting a sprig from the bride's bouquet when the party returned from church. The planting, done always by a bridesmaid and never by the bride, brought happiness to the couple and early marriage to the planter if the slip 'took'—a likely outcome since the plant is notoriously easy to strike. Gloucestershire bridesmaids carried *Achillea ptarmica*, 'shirt buttons', or 'seven years' love', in their posies. Country music of pipes and fiddles went with the party, and in the Isle of Man 'the tune, *The Black and the Grey*, and no other . . . was ever used at weddings.' Often the party prudently circled the church three times sunwise for luck, before entering, and since it was unlucky for the church clock to strike during the marriage service, a short wait outside might be required.

Many wedding customs derive from ancient passage and fertility rites, otherwise forgotten, and symbolism crept in. To mark the severance with their old lives, bride and bridegroom leapt over a bench in Cleveland and, this done, a gun charged with feathers was fired, symbolising a wish that nothing harder might ever fall upon them. In Somerset the church path is still chained with a rope of flowers and in the Forest of Dean children tie the churchyard gate shut and only open it when the bridegroom throws them money. At Chaddleworth, Berkshire, whichever of the couple set foot first over the steep church step would be master for life, and amused spectators saw speeding feet as the door was approached. Devon brides were greeted by an old woman offering a fertility gift of hazelnuts, and in the country a good nut year is still thought a good one for babies—'plenty of nuts, plenty of cradles', is the prediction. At Nottinghamshire weddings, wheat was thrown to the cheerful shout of 'Bread for life and pudding for ever!'

Hazelnuts for the bride

Shoes, as ancient good-luck symbols, are still thrown at weddings. At a Leicestershire village wedding about 1860 (where the celebrations went on for nearly a week), the bride's brother threw a battered hobnailed tramp's boot (found in the road), right over the bridal carriage into the rhododendrons. In full bridal rig the bridesmaids plunged after it, for she who retrieved it would be next to marry. Once found, the boot hung for the day from a white satin ribbon in the house.[9]

The clergyman, too, had his ordeals. In Yorkshire the parson, however retiring, was expected to kiss the bride at the conclusion of the ceremony. One clergyman noticing a loitering bridal party, was told: 'Please, Sir, ye've no kissed Mollie.' And up to about 1846 at Barmby Moor, the parson had to dash to the vestry at the very moment of finishing the service, amid a well-aimed shower of hassocks and service-books, hurled at him by high-spirited guests.

Northern country weddings were marked by boisterous races,

especially for the luck-bringing bride's garter. At Tudor weddings the garter was removed by a jovial company when the bride was bedded, but by the seventeenth century, attempts were sometimes made to snatch it even at the altar itself, and the bride might be forced to scream out or even be thrown down in the scramble, before the jubilant captors carried their trophy high above their heads round the church. To prevent what an outraged Yorkshire clergyman called, 'this very indecent assault' garters began to be given from bosoms and genteel country brides sometimes substituted long white ribbons (called garters) and silk handkerchiefs, to be raced for after the wedding. The lively older-fashioned race for the garter survived into the last century in some villages: Mrs Peary of Sand Hill Farm, Picton, Yorkshire, aged about seventy-three in 1898, told Richard Blakeborough that running for the bride's garter was common in her mother's time, although the ribbon was more usual in hers. While she could not recall a specific instance of 'flinging the stocking' she had certainly heard of it.

The young men would clatter from the church, leap upon their horses and ride full-pelt 'for the bride's door'. There the kneeling winner of the race waited for the bride's arrival; she raised her skirt and he claimed his prize. In 1898 Richard Blakeborough noted that while the race was less common than formerly it had nevertheless been run within the past five years in the North Riding, and an eye-witness had told him of another garter race earlier in the century:

Why, as recently as 1820, Lady ——, a great stickler after old customs, on stepping from her bridal coach, enquired, who had won the race. 'Ah did, My Lady,' answered one of the stable-lads. Ascending the steps, Her Ladyship stepped half-over the threshold, calling out to the lad, 'Come, Tom, and claim your prize,' adding, as she raised her silken gown, 'I intend to be properly married and to have the luck I am entitled to.' Then turning to the young fellow, smiling, she added, 'Take it off, Tom, and give it to your sweetheart, and may it bring luck to both of you.'[10]

Riding for the kail, a bowl of spiced cabbage broth, was another leading wedding race and sometimes the bride gave the competitors a kiss before they started. The liveliness of northern weddings had to be experienced to be believed; the Rev J. Barmby spoke feelingly of a Yorkshire Dales wedding:

> ... nothing can be imagined comparable to it in wildness and obstreperous mirth. The bride and bridegroom may possibly be a little subdued, but their friends are like men bereft of reason. They career round the bridal party like Arabs of the desert, galloping over ground on which, in cooler moments, they would hesitate even to walk a horse—shouting all the time, and firing volleys from the guns they carry with them ... In the higher parts of Northumberland, as well as on the other side of the Border, the scene is, if possible, still more wild.[11]

The firing of guns, customary at northern weddings, would seem to be a relic of the fight accompanying primitive bride-capture.

Further south, at Claybrook, Leicestershire, in the early eighteenth century (the last witness was still alive in 1791), the race for the bride-cake started the moment the bride left for her new home. The cake was set upon a pole about twelve feet high and the young men galloped ahead to reach the pole first and to knock the cake down.[12]

Pieces of wedding cake passed through the wedding ring and put under pillows as 'dreaming bread' induced visions of future husbands. At Sussex weddings to ensure the couple's fertility and prosperity, a 'bride's pie' with thick crust and containing a hen full of hard-boiled eggs, was always baked. No wedding was complete without it.[13] And in the North Riding 'hen silver' was given to poor neighbours to drink the bride's health, and a hen commonly taken to the newly-weds' house to cackle, for luck.

Once the feast was over and the sack posset drunk ('sack will make a man lusty, and sugar will make him kind'), the wedding ring might be dropped into the posset-cup for whoever found it would be first to marry. The bride was escorted to her chamber by the bridesmaids who put her to bed, removing all pins from her clothes, symbolising the removal of the prick of care and misfortune. If any were overlooked nothing would go right, and if the bridesmaids kept even one they would not marry. The company stamped noisily upstairs to the bashful couple to 'fling the stocking'. The bride's stockings were seized by the young men and the bridegroom's by the girls and each group sat at the bed's foot to fling the stockings backwards towards the bedded pair, to fall, for early success in marriage, on the bride if thrown by the men, or on the bridegroom if thrown by the girls. These cheerful customs were at their peak from about 1600–1750, but they faded with the greater sense of propriety of later years. But the old wedding activities left their mark. A writer in the Toronto *Globe and Mail*, 23 June 1911, suggested that 'throwing the bride's bouquet', seen all over North America—whoever catches it will be first to marry—might well have sprung from the older custom of flinging the stocking.

In Devon in the nineteenth century, doorsteps were well scrubbed when the bride left her father's house, showing her acceptance of a new home, and in Yorkshire a kettleful of boiling water was poured over the step and the bride wetted her shoes in it to induce a happy marriage for another of the company, which would be arranged before the water was dry. The bride must enter her new home by the front door, where once the fireirons were put into her hands as the emblems of her role. A stumble as she enters is extremely ill-omened, and to avoid this disaster brides are carried over thresholds from Cornwall to Connecticut.

The bidden-wedding, bride-wain or bride-ale followed the wedding, and was a great social event. Once the newly-married couple had collected corn and wood from friends by wain or waggon (in eighteenth-century Yorkshire the wain was drawn by as many as twenty pairs of oxen with beribboned horns, and friends and well-wishers threw gifts of furniture into it as it rolled through the villages). Sometimes the bride sold ale to give the couple a good financial start in life, and the custom persisted in one form or another. North Country neighbours rode to bidden-weddings with saddle-bags heavy with gifts of flour, poultry, eggs, bacon and butter, and after a sociable day left as much as £200 in a discreetly placed plate for a popular young couple. Sometimes furniture and household articles (the origin of the American 'shower') were brought by friends just before the wedding. Canon J. C. Atkinson found that in the farmhouses of his Yorkshire Dales village of Danby-in-Cleveland about 1850, the fine old black oak cabinets with folding doors, carved panels and knob feet, which had formed part of the wedding presents, were invariably called 'bride-wains'.[14]

The *Cumberland Packet* had a special column for the announcement of bidden-weddings:

> George Hayto who married Anne, the daughter of Joseph and Dinah Colin of Crosby Mill, purposes having a Bride-wain at his house at Crosby, near Maryport, on Thursday, 7th of May, next (1789), where he will be happy to see his friends and well-wishers; for whose amusement there will be a variety of races, wrestling matches, &c. . . . The prizes will be—a saddle, two bridles, a pair of *gands d'amour*, gloves which, whoever wins, is sure to be married within the twelvemonths; a girdle (*ceinture de Venus*), possessing qualities not to be described; and many other articles, sports and pastimes, too numerous to mention . . .

and another invitation began:

> Suspend for a day your cares and your labours,
> And come to the wedding, kind friends and good neighbours.

and ended:

> *Nota Bene*: You'll be pleased to observe that the day,
> Of this grand bridal pomp is the thirtieth of May,
> When 'tis hop'd that the sun, to enliven the sight,
> Like the flambeau of Hymen will deign to burn bright.

MARRIED LIFE

The mob custom of 'rough music', 'skimmington' or 'riding the stang' survived into this century to expose matrimonial offences such as adultery, nagging or beating, or to mock a husband who permitted himself to be henpecked, according to the convention that any man or woman not playing a sexually appropriate or acceptable role was dangerous to communal fertility. Villagers gathered in night procession at the offender's house, beating old pots and pans, and shouting insulting rhymes. Sometimes a boy rode a pole or stang in mimicry of the victim. Walter Rose, writing in 1943, remembered that in a particular Haddenham cottage there hung an old copper 'rough-musicking' horn, regarded as common property. Misbehaviour condemned by the village was followed by its hoarse blast and the sound of hobnailed boots in the lanes as villagers gathered to administer the punishment.[15]

When a spry young blacksmith of West Lulworth, Dorset, married an old, ill-favoured but wealthy woman, the villagers showed their disapproval by leaving on the doorstep their wedding present of a cradle, and stuffing a bag of straw down the chimney to make the newly-weds' first hours together as uncomfortable as possible. The unpleasantness of rough music was seen as late as 1935 in Chapman Camp, British Columbia, after the wedding of an unpopular school-teacher.[16] The victim seldom recovered his honour in neighbours' eyes and often left the village, as his tormentors had hoped he would, thus removing the menace of his irregularity from the group. Public penance, ecclesiastical discipline in use until the last century and imposed especially for adultery, was another harrowing experience for a vic-tim, who on a Sunday morning must stand before the congregation to confess his or her sin, bareheaded and barelegged, wrapped from head to foot in a white sheet, white wand in hand. Many condemned this heartless practice.

If the marriage foundered the wife could always be 'sold' in what amounted to informal divorce, approved by at least sections of society. Great surprise was expressed among poorer people when a West Riding man, Joshua Jackson, was imprisoned in 1837 for attempting such a sale. Joseph Thomson, a Cumberland farmer unhappily married for three years, sold his wife in Carlisle market on 7 April 1832, with a straw halter round her neck. She was offered with the uninviting testimonial that she was a 'born serpent' and a 'domestic curse' but, fairly enough, with a view to sale, her good qualities were also speci-fied: she could milk cows, read novels, make butter, scold the maids and sing, and she was sold for twenty shillings and a Newfoundland dog.

The payment of money and the provision of the halter was felt to give perfect legality to the matter. When an objection was raised over the registration of his 'wife's' death at Lew Trenchard, Devon, about 1843 Henry Frise retorted 'Her's my wife, as sure as if we was spliced at the altar, for and because I paid half a crown and never took off the halter till her was in my house.'[17] Sometimes unimaginative market inspectors, bent on duty, attempted to charge tolls on these sales. At Brighton in 1826, one shilling was levied and when the magistrates challenged the inspector, he stolidly quoted the bye-laws—'Any article not enumerated in these byelaws pays one shilling.'

THE GRAVE

One of the strangest death-divination rituals was 'watching in the church porch', often on St Mark's Eve, when the intrepid watcher would see all those to die in the parish within the coming year pass in ghostly procession before him. A young carpenter in Monk-Okehampton, Devon, saw two persons pass, followed by his own wraith and in terror fled home to take to his bed. Vainly did rector and doctor remonstrate with him, and despite all reassurances he died within two weeks. Less alarmingly, about 1826, old Benn Barr of Helpston, Northamptonshire, who watched every year and professed to know the fate of everyone in the village, was reported quite ready to find a favourable verdict for the timid, for the inducement of a few pence. Watching must be observed for three years before results would be obtained but once begun it must continue for life. On Exmoor the only safe place for the watcher to stand was under the lych-gate and even this might not protect him during the dangerous work. Household ashes were smoothly riddled on to the hearth on St Mark's Eve and in the morning would bear the footprint of any member of the family to die that year. On the Isle of Man an in-turning footprint meant a coming birth but one pointing towards the door a death. Chaff-riddling was another procedure, carried out at midnight in northern barns. With barndoor open the enquirers passed the chaff through the sieve in turn and should a coffin pass by, the person working at the time would die within the year; a Malton, Yorkshire, woman used the method about 1860 and though her companions saw nothing, she saw two coffin-bearers pass and died soon afterwards.

As the moment of death drew near all house locks, bolts, doors and windows were opened to ease the passing. 'It originates from the belief which formerly prevailed that the soul flew out of the mouth of the dying in the likeness of a bird,' commented *The Athenaeum* on 17 October 1846. But the past tense was premature for 'My grandmother told me,' writes Mrs Baker, 'that when my grandfather died at Canterbury in 1893, she distinctly saw his soul fly away in the form of a white bird.'

It was commonly believed that no one could die easily on a bed stuffed with game or pigeon feathers, however few. A Sussex labourer remarked about 1850, 'Look at poor Muster S——, how hard he were a dying; poor soul, he could not die any way, till neighbour Puttick found out how it wer,—"Muster S——," says he, "ye be lying on geame feathers, mon, surely;" and so he were. So we took'n out o'bed and laid'n on the floor, and he *pretty soon died then*!' For a sick man to lie under a crossbeam of the house also delayed death, and a clergyman near Cullompton, Devon, recalled that at one death-bed which seemed inexplicably prolonged, a relative noticed a beam concealed in the floor above; the bed was moved and death followed swiftly. When the end was inevitable, the passing bell was rung and prayers said for the dying (although the bell's original purpose was more probably to drive away evil spirits than to invite prayers). The traditional Nine Tailors (or Tellers), nine strokes of a bell for a man and six for a woman, followed by one stroke for each year of the deceased's age, are still rung in some village churches.

It was common practice to put a dish of salt upon the body after death, some maintained to prevent bodily changes, although the use of salt, when earth or stones would have been far more readily available, clearly points to a protective rite. Several counties tell of the farmer's boy at the hiring-fair who was asked by a prospective employer why he had left his last job. 'Well,' said the boy, 'the old sow died and we salted she and et she. Then the old cow died and we salted she and et she. Then the old 'ooman died and I see'd master goo upstairs with the bowl o' salt, so I cum right on down.'

Mirrors were covered with a white cloth after a death, lest the next to die be seen reflected in them. Clocks stopped spontaneously at their owner's death or were deliberately stopped until the funeral was over, to prevent further deaths. To stimulate the wool trade an Act of 1678 (which remained in force until 1814, although it had fallen in disuse long before repeal), required an affidavit, entered in the *Wool Book*, that the body had been 'buried in woollen'—shroud, chincloth, gloves and cravat must all be of wool. Cotton shrouds eventually took the place of woollen, but the changeover was not without difficulties. The writer's grandmother, who died in 1943, aged 94, told of an ancestor apprenticed to a Reading linen-draper into whose shop an elderly farmer came to buy a nightshirt. Rummaging round with a candle in the dark storeroom, the young man found what seemed exactly the right garment. The old man departed well pleased with his purchase, and only the horrified laughter of the other shopmen told the novice that he had, in fact, sold the customer one of the new-fangled cotton shrouds.

Often the dead person's most cherished goods, such as pipe or beer-mug, were laid in the coffin beside him, a relic of an age-old idea that goods might be needed in the after-life. In *Under a Suffolk Sky*, Allan Jobson writes of a Suffolk man, fond of his grandfather clock, who asked that it should serve as his coffin, but his shrewd relations, pleading with cause that there was insufficient room for both corpse and clock-works (by Thomas Tompion), prudently sold the latter at a good profit, leaving the case alone to go to the churchyard with its owner.

Eccentric burials led to local legends. 'Mad' Jack Fuller, squire of Brightling, Sussex, requested to be buried in his pyramidal tomb in Brightling churchyard in 1833 seated at a table bearing a roast pheasant and a bottle of port. The floor of the tomb was sprinkled with broken glass to 'keep Satan out' until the owner was ready to take possession. A troublesome Culmstock woman was buried upside-down, a favourite trick of sextons with notorious corpses. Local Devonian debate had decided that this was the safest position for her for 'her can on'y diggy down'ards' and Miss Ellen Nash, who died in 1963 aged 83, recalled that her father, village sexton of Aldermaston for over fifty years, had joined villagers in piling stones on the grave of Maria Hale, the notorious local witch, to ensure that she, too, could never rise again.[18]

FUNERAL AND FEAST

Up to the twentieth century invitations to funerals or 'siding-bys' were taken round by dozens. Lancashire mourners were often met at the door by a prim female in black with white apron, who offered spiced wine, a slice of currant bread and a bun. The mourners (each wearing the sprig of rosemary left by the 'bidder', which would later be dropped into the grave), were invited to take a last look at the deceased and to present a shilling to the relations who sat conveniently at the coffin head to receive it. Many mourners snatched the chance to talk about farming and to do a little quiet business before the procession moved off.

Major Fairfax-Blakeborough writes that he is still 'bidden' to North Riding funerals and that while the cake, wines and spirits once offered before the coffin was 'lifted' and the pipes, tobacco and gin on the table afterwards, are no longer seen, a good selection of hymns and a hearty Yorkshire tea are confidently anticipated. In earlier years 'wakes' and 'arvals' (with arval cakes), plenty to eat and drink, and amusements for the mourners, were common; 'wet wakes', carried enthusiastically to North America,[19] became excuses for night-long drinking bouts. Sometimes the corpse was considerately propped up against the wall so that it, too, might join in the fun and many a coffin served as a table for a sociable game of cards.

'Doles' were common. In 1790 one man reported that there were 432 inhabitants in Stathern-in-Framland Hundred in Leicestershire. Should he not know? for had he not carried round the 'dole loaves' sent out after the death of a villager and given to all without reference to age or circumstances, the rejection of which was the grossest disrespect? At richer Lancashire funerals up to about 1850, a penny dole was added to the refreshments and some, it was said, 'would rather go seven or eight miles to a penny dole, than earn sixpence in the same time by laudable industry'.[20]

Preparations for the funeral feast were often made far in advance. One Dorset squire enquiring after a sick labourer he had not expected to find alive, was told by the man's wife that her husband was very much stronger, for the night before he had got out of bed, come downstairs and helped himself to a good plateful of funeral ham, standing ready for his departure from this world. 'We buried him on ham' was the cottager's proud boast, and in Guernsey 'Màngier la tchesse à quiqu'un'—'to eat a person's ham'—was synonymous with attending his funeral.[21]

A funeral between New and Old Christmas meant a death in the parish for every month of the coming year and if the number of mourners were odd, he who walked alone would be next to die. Front doors are rarely opened in the country, but the corpse must leave this way, feet foremost, or its soul will be imperilled; many a battle has taken place with rusty hinges at rural funerals. The corpse must be carried in the direction of the sun, at least into the churchyard, and many processions made a careful swing round the churchyard wall to make the correct approach. For a funeral procession to meet the sun on his course was most unlucky and was 'going to be buried the back way'.

At the funeral of a Claybrook, Leicestershire, yeoman or farmer at the end of the eighteenth century (typical of many rural funerals) the clergyman in canonicals led the way, followed by the relations, two by two, by sex, arms linked. The body of a young man was attended by six girls in white, as pall-bearers, and young men in white gloves and hatbands escorted the body of a girl.[22] Black was customary at the deaths of older persons, and at one Suffolk squire's funeral (enshrined in local memory as a particularly impressive affair) sixty-five hatbands, scarves and pairs of gloves were handed out to mourners; the general conclusion was 'the greater the number of hatbands needed the greater the respect'. At one time (and more than a shadow of the custom remains), mourners attended church on the Sunday following a funeral—Mourning Sunday—to hear the funeral sermon. The Rev F. B. M. Camm, writing in April 1902, reported that in his parish of Monkton Wyld, Dorset, the mourners came to church and remained seated throughout the whole proceedings with handkerchiefs held dramatically to their faces, and apparently oblivious of the progress of the service.[23]

A well-documented custom of primitive origin was 'sin-eating', which perhaps underlay the elaborate funeral feasts. John Aubrey's much-quoted account states:

> In the county of Hereford, was an old custom at funeralls to hire poor people, who were to take upon them the sinnes of the party deceased. One of them (he was a long, leane, ugly, lamentable poor raskal), I remember, lived in a cottage on Rosse Highway. The manner was, that when the corpse was brought out of the house, and layd on the biere, a

loafe of bread was brought out, and delivered to the sinne eater, over the corpse, as also a mazar bowle, of maple, full of beer (which he was to drink up), and sixpence in money; in consideration whereof he took upon him, *ipso facto*, all the sinnes of the defunct, and freed him or her from walking after they were dead.

Maiden garlands were seen at the funerals of girls and youths. About 1820 Mary Hill was killed in a belfry accident at Springthorpe Church, Lincolnshire and at her funeral three girls in white carried in the funeral procession three white paper crowns and pairs of paper gloves which were afterwards hung in the church.[24] There were many designs; gold or silver wire hoops were sometimes covered with

Maiden garlands at Ashford-in-the-Water church, Derbyshire, about 1860

paper rosettes, dyed horn and silk flowers, and suspended within was a pair of white paper gloves, inscribed with the name and age of the deceased. Ribbons of crimped paper and gilded shells or birds' eggs completed the decoration, with perhaps an hourglass, redolent of man's mortality. (Hourglasses were still distributed among mourners at Georgian funerals.) The custom of maiden garlands survives at Abbotts Ann, Hampshire, where the garlands in the church date from 1716 to the present.

6

The
Country Church

Today the country church plays a diminished role, but in the age of faith it was at the heart of country life. Wakes and ales, Rogationtide ceremonies, saints' days, welldressings, rushbearings, tithing and charities influenced the whole spiritual and temporal life of the community, and made the church's feasts and festivals those of the village itself. The pre-Reformation power of the church took several centuries to fade and its faint shadow may be traced to this day.

CUSTOMS OF THE CHURCH

Until the Tithe Commutation Act of 1836 the parson could take his tithes in kind; they partially supported him and were a fruitful cause of ill-feeling in country parishes. In Wiltshire an old labourer stuck a green bough in the vicar's shocks as the sheaves were stood up in the field, to mark those which would later be collected by the vicarage cart. The tenth pig, the tenth sheaf and the tenth sack of apples were taken in good years or bad, although not without protest. A country joke (perpetuated in china groups for the Georgian farm chimney piece) tells of the woman who offered the alarmed clergyman her tenth baby instead of the sow's tenth piglet, which her husband had in firm grasp. 'Just like the parson's barn' was a cynical Dorset saying, meaning never so full that it could not take more. Farmers' feelings were well expressed in the old song, roared out with relish at many a village gathering:

We've cheated the parson, we'll cheat him again,
For why should the blockhead have one in ten?

Once collected the tithes in kind were stored in great barns, of which a number, including the fourteenth-century barn once part of the Lacock Abbey buildings and the Great Barn at Great Coxwell, Berkshire, now both National Trust properties, remain. Wise parsons soothed the farmers' ruffled feelings with a jovial tithe-audit dinner. On 5 February 1878, Parson Kilvert superintended such a dinner at Bredwardine Vicarage, Herefordshire. Many of the fifty tithepayers there were small farmers paying only a few pence, but they made the most of their opportunity and, probably in a spirit of revenge, made a hearty meal of the bread, cheese and beer provided. Payers arrived until six o'clock, and an hour later parson and farmers sat down to dinner together: to turkey, roast beef, jugged hare and beefsteak pie, with apple tart, mince-pies, blancmange, plum pudding, cheese and fruit to follow.[1]

Farmers were invited to tithe breakfasts held at Eastbourne parsonage on the first three Sundays in August, to enjoy sirloin of beef, ham, Sussex cheese, strong ale and Geneva. For every waggon the farm owned, two servants were sent to a similar meal in the barn.[2]

A wake or feast celebrated the feast of the saint to whom the village church was dedicated. Once a solemn occasion, a night spent in prayer in the church, it later became the annual holiday of the district. Reverence slipped away with the years. The Claybrook historian wrote in 1791:

> The people of this neighbourhood are much attached to the celebration of wakes; and on the annual return of those festivals, the cousins assemble from all quarters, fill the church on Sunday, and celebrate Monday with feasting, with musick, and with dancing. The spirit of old English hospitality is conspicuous among the farmers on those occasions, but with the lower sort of people . . . the return of the wake never fails to produce a week, at least, of idleness, intoxication, and riot.[3]

At Great Coxwell, Berkshire on the feast of St Giles, a fiddler came from Bristol to set up his dancing booth under the light of naphtha flares (one villager boasted that he had danced his shoes right off his feet), and a festival meal of cut-and-come-again ham and plum pudding was seen in every cottage. At Long Itchington, Warwickshire, a stuffed bacon chine stood 'in cut' on every sideboard for Trinity Wake Week, and wake-pudding of bread and butter, eggs, milk, sugar, suet, currants and peel was eaten by all. At Radley feast, folk were sustained by an enormous Berkshire plum-pudding made by the landlord's wife at the Bowyers Arms and by her ginger beer, and old Radley folk still call early August 'feast time', although the feast did not really survive World War I.

A wake at Welford, Warwickshire

In Cheshire frumenty was the principal wake dish, and at West Houghton, knowledgeable visitors were attracted from miles around by the succulent flat pork pasties baked for the day. Contests were many: at Audlem on 5 October 1812, wake sports included such lively events as eating hasty pudding, smoking tobacco and a hot tea-drinking by three old women. A prize was awarded to the first person to finish a plate of hot porridge and treacle, eaten sitting on the church steps, and the first man to get drunk at the wake was dubbed 'Mayor of Audlem' for the year. Feasts and wakes are no more but their shadows survive in the rural calendar, for the old dates are still often named as excellent planting days.

At the churchhouse, still sometimes existing as a cottage or inn at the churchyard gate, the churchwardens sold ale on Sundays, Whitsun and Easter to raise money for church and poor. Taking advantage of the often excellent equipment of spits, crockery and fireplaces, parishioners 'met and were merry, and gave their charity. The young people were there, too, and had dancing, bowling, shooting at butts, &c., the ancients sitting gravely by, and looking on. All things were civil and without scandal,' wrote Aubrey pleasantly of his grandfather's day at Kington St Michael in Wiltshire.[4]

Walking the parish boundaries at Rogationtide was an essential part of parish administration before maps and literacy were common-place, done, partially at least, to make clear to parish officers their boundaries for burial and poor-law purposes. At the boundary marks (a tree, stone or pond) the parson paused to give thanks for the fruits of the earth and to read the gospel. (Field names such as Gospel, Amen or Paternoster often point to former significance as marks.) The company, carrying peeled willow wands, then turned to the boys and, more or less severely according to period, beat and bumped them or pushed them in a nearby stream, all excellent reminders of boundaries, and to add to the memorability, bread, cheese and ale followed. At Clifton Reynes, Buckinghamshire, reported the charity commissioners about 1842, a pasture-field called Kites provided a small loaf, a piece of cheese and ale 'on the feast of Stephen', as a telling bribe to every person who walked the bounds in Rogation week. One Buckinghamshire boundary lay right under a farm oven, into which a boy, having won this dubious honour by lot, was annually pushed. One year the mistress of the house was preparing to bake as the party approached and the oven was full of blazing faggots. The delighted boys shouted 'Tom Smith is to go into the oven' and Tom, expecting to be roasted alive, fled home shrieking. Another boy was persuaded to climb over the oven's roof to fulfil requirements. Clipping or embracing, an emblematic expression of affection for the church, continues in a number of villages, including Painswick, Gloucestershire, where, on the Sunday nearest 19 September, children with garlands process through the streets of the village, and joining hands completely encircle the church in a simple dance.

Hay, once laid on clay or stone floors for cleanliness and warmth, is still strewed in a few churches at the patronal festival. A field at Old Weston, Huntingdonshire, was bequeathed to the parish clerk on condition that it is mowed for strewing in July, to quieten the squeaking boots worn by villagers on the feast day and a meadow of three roods at Wingrave, Buckinghamshire, given by a woman lost but saved by Wingrave bells, provides hay (as well as hassocks and carpets) on the Sunday after the feast of St Peter, Feast Sunday.

The ceremonial strewing of rushes, valued for their sweet smell, developed into the more sophisticated practice of rush-bearing. A mid-nineteenth-century account of rush-bearing at Runcorn and Warburton, Cheshire, noted great bolts of rushes decorated with oakleaves and bound to a cart; on the Saturday evening, holding garlands of artificial flowers and tinsel, men rode on the last load, and the rushcart was drawn through the parish by young men or by spirited horses decorated with ribbons and bells. Morris dancers attended, dancing the long morris during the procession and the cross morris when a halt was called. The party left rushes and garlands at the church to hang until the next rush-bearing.[5] At Ambleside and Grasmere on the Saturday nearest St Oswald's Day, 5 August, since rushes are no longer needed as floor-coverings, dressed 'rush-bearings' in traditional shapes such as Moses-in-the-bulrushes, harp, and St Oswald's hand and crown are carried in procession.

Well-dressing is especially associated with the Derbyshire villages of Tissington, Tideswell, Wirksworth, Buxton, Ashford and Eyam. Wells are dressed at dates from Ascensiontide to mid-August, and Tissington boasts that the festival has been held without interruption since the drought of 1615 (some say since the Black Death), when the wells never failed and farmers brought cows ten miles for water. Today a brief service is held at each of the five wells in the village. During the past hundred years well-dressing has become an intricate rural craft at which local families show great skill. There is keen

An eighteenth-century rushbearing

rivalry to produce the most beautiful designs; a boarded framework is coated with damp clay into which flower petals, berries, leaves, moss, feathers, seeds and cones (all materials must be natural) are pressed to form pictures, usually of biblical subjects, which glow softly for days before fading. An observer of about 1860 saw yellow field ranunculus (buttercups), violets, daisies, primroses, flowering currant, mountain ash and yew berries used, and noted that in the happy spirit of the day, cottagers vied with each other to boil kettles for visitors picnicking on the green. A newspaper account of the Buxton dressing of 1846 noted that the season was early and suitable wildflowers were scarce but that roses, pansies, foxgloves, columbines, daisies and white clover were blended with the scarlet berries of the rowan, with box and fir borders and some *Fuchsia gracilis*, to make the designs. 'About two o'clock the morris-dancers started on their round, accompanied by the Duke of Devonshire's and the Pilsley bands, but their graceful evolutions were frequently interrupted by showers of rain. About six o'clock the clouds all cleared away, and we had as fine an evening as ever shone from the heavens . . . when the weather became clear nearly every public-house had its own knot of dancers.'[6]

CHARITIES

Hundreds of ancient charities continue, some now in the form of cash gifts, rather than in kind. Food (plum-puddings, mince pies, beef, tobacco and ale were favourite bequests), money and clothing formed the main components of doles, which reflected their founders' kindly concern for the less fortunate of the community—and often their ingenuity. Henry Green of Melbourne, for example, left lands in 1679 to provide *green* waistcoats on 21 December, Gooding Day, to be worn by four poor widows on Christmas Day. This idea must have tickled the fancy of Thomas Gray, for twelve years later he made a similar bequest for the provision of *grey* waistcoats and coats.

A peapicking charity continues at Sawston, Cambridgeshire, where in 1554, John Huntingdon ordained that whoever held his manor in years to come, should plant two acres of white peas every year in the Linton Field, to be picked on a day chosen by the trustees. Picking now occupies a July day from midday to dusk. It was once led by the 'queen of the gleaners', although despite this supervision, an observer of 1842 noted that 'A complete scene of scramble and confusion ensues attended with occasional conflicts.'[7] The Duke of Marlborough, a large landowner in the neighbourhood, provided two cows for the Waddesdon poor, to be kept by the tenant of Lodge Hill Farm. In 1833 milk from one cow only was received daily by 22 parishioners in rotation, for in 1825 the tenant had refused to keep the second cow, claiming as insufficient the allowance of £10 from his grace. If the 'alms cow' died or went dry, the responsibility for finding a replacement was the tenant's. Mr Cecil Atkins told the writer in 1972 that he well remembers villagers with jugs going to the home-farm dairy for the milk, for when Baron Ferdinand de Rothschild bought Lodge Hill Farm to build Waddesdon Manor, he and later his sister Alice continued the old dole from the estate farm.

In 1837 the charity commissioners reported that until the enclosure of Swaffham Bulbeck an acre of land in the open field called Plum Cake Acre had provided income from which the tenant of Abbey Farm was to give a slice of plum cake and a glass of ale to all parishioners who applied for them. Every third year the land was dispastured under the open-field system and the gift lapsed.

Gleaning or leasing was a practical privilege acknowledged as a customary right by all, but apparently without legal basis although no farmer, whatever his private feelings, could have faced the village hostility had he forbidden it. By the Fenland code of fifty years ago, farmers would lay five sheaves on the hedge to intimate that the gate would be opened to gleaners at five o'clock next morning; an Oxfordshire man, aged 79, writing about 1957, remembered that if a few stacked sheaves were left in the field it was 'not carried' and closed to gleaners.[8] Sometimes the relatively well-to-do made use of the privilege; the writer's great-grandmother, wife of the police sergeant at Canterbury, Kent, was not too proud to take her seven children gleaning; their corn (enough for the whole winter) was ground by the miller, who kept a little flour for his trouble.

At Little Shelford, gleaners were led to work by their chosen 'queen', who sat in state all day in the field, 'shoeing' new gleaners, signalling when work must begin and cease, arranging meal breaks and seeing that all enjoyed fair shares. At Rempston, Leicestershire, about 1859, she was carried to the field in a chair, a crown of wild flowers and corn upon her head; her instructions ended with the words 'May you glean in peace'. And showing that charity was often an unsung matter for the individual heart, Dame Tanner of Avon Mill, Wiltshire, known for her kindly ways, gave gleaning cakes to each poor person who brought gleaned corn to be ground at her mill, as a reward for thrift and industry. Gleaning for the family larder died out from 1900 to 1914, more perhaps through the introduction of mechanical harvesters which left few ears behind than from alleviation of want, although improvements in rural wages naturally played their part. A little gleaning for hens and pigs has always continued, particularly during World War II.

Clothing was another customary gift; two cottages let at Hampstead Norris, Berkshire, provided blue greatcoats for men and white felt petticoats for women. Up to the 1880s and later these were distributed to elderly villagers on Whit-Sunday and if Whitsun were late and the weather hot, many were the grumbles from the uncomfortable recipients who had to wear them to church on that day. Barley from certain lands in Little Coxwell, Berkshire, provided revenue used to teach two poor children to read, write and cast accounts, and a kindly benefactor at Winkfield bequeathed £200 in 1778 to pay the expenses of those too poor to afford the marriage fees. With admirable candour John Rudge of Trysull, Staffordshire, in 1725 left twenty shillings a year to pay a poor man to go about the church during the sermon to wake sleepers, for a hard week's work in the fields made this opportunity for slumber irresistible.

CHURCH AND CHURCHYARD

A body of local rhymes, which more or less frankly point out defects in church, parson, bells and congregation emphasise earlier village rivalries.

> Sauket church, crook'd steeple,
> Drunken parson, wicked people,

said of Saltcote or Playden in Sussex is a typical example, and

> Aynho bell metal,
> Souldern tin kettle,

spoke of the much-prized village bells, sources of great satisfaction to their owners and of envy to neighbours. Friendly rivalry may still creep in: the bells of Langford Budville, Somerset, are rung on Midsummer Night to 'drive the devil over to Thorne St Margaret', and on St Thomas à Becket's Day, 7 July (Midsummer Day Old Style), Thorne St Margaret rings her bells to drive him back again.[9] Change-ringing is a peculiarly English art and ringing-chamber walls often bear painted Georgian and Victorian inscriptions to epic peals of the past— Grandsire Triples, Stedman Triples or Kent Bob Majors—perhaps rung as wedding compliments to long-dead squires and their brides, by blacksmith, miller, farmer or publican. In Nottinghamshire villages, the commemorative marks on the belfry walls were called 'cakes' or 'cheeses' after the gifts customary on these occasions. At East Drayton, the bridal party walked back to church after the wedding breakfast with the best man carrying in a basket covered with a white cloth, a plum loaf of 6 or 8 pounds weight, a knife, a cheese and money for beer. These were presented to the oldest bellringer for distribution. And the belfry at Aldington, Warwickshire, was decorated with bones from beef and mutton joints, commemorating weddings of prominent parishioners and plainly hinting that further feasts for the bellringers on such occasions would be welcome.[10] Sometimes a 'dumb' or muffled peal was rung on the death of a bellringer, and in 1817 Bromley ringers rang 5,040 changes of Grandsire Triples for William Chapman, one of their number for forty-three years. The bells themselves were legendary and when Lavenham tenor bell was cast, several Suffolk gentlemen drank to 'Church and King' before throwing their silver tankards into the molten metal to sweeten the bell's note.

'Ringing of bells is one of their great delights, especially in the country,' wrote Henri Misson de Valbourg about 1690; it is an art which survives in full measure and the old ringers' rules are still obeyed. At Frodsham, Cheshire:

> From faults observe you Ringers well,
> Ring true and don't o'er turn your Bell;
> On each default by him that's made,
> Down sixpence surely shall be paid;
> Swear not in this most sacred place,
> Here come not but with aweful grace
> And who'er rings with Spur or Hat
> Must sixpence pay or forfeit that.[11]

Churchbells are still the most arresting sound in village consciousness and still mark special events—the coming of Christmas and the New Year, weddings and funerals. Up to the last century the potato or pudding bell was often rung to warn housewives that it was time to put the Sunday dinner on. Villages rang, and in a few cases still ring, curfews. At Barton, Lincolnshire, an old lady benighted on the Wolds was directed to safety by the curfew bell and she gave a piece of land to the parish clerk of the day, provided a bell was rung from seven to eight o'clock each evening from the time the first load of barley was carried until Shrove Tuesday. Bells rang at 5 am to rouse harvesters and others at 7 pm to mark the end of their day. In Cheshire it was said that church bells should ring three times over the stooked corn before it was carried, and careful farmers cut their corn at the end of the week so that the grain should have maximum benefit from the bells with the minimum delay to themselves.[12] At Louth the gatherum bell signalled the start of peapicking. Other bells joyfully marked the completion of harvest. Gleaning bells began and ended the day in the fields, and at West Deeping the parish clerk refused this service when the gleaners would not pay 2d for it. Ringers at Harlington received a succulent leg of pork from the income of Pork Acre, provided they rang a peal on 5 November, Guy Fawkes Day.

Church clocks, closely concerned with the measurement of village days, were full of omens; for example, if the clock struck while the text was being given, a death would follow in the parish that week. Quire, Bellrope or Lamplands are fieldnames showing that the income from the lands supported various items of the church fabric; Clock Holt Wood, for example, has from time immemorial provided funds for the winding and repairing of the church clock at Haslingfield, Cambridgeshire.[13]

Despite their sanctity, it was often felt wise to protect churches with charms and amulets as though they were houses or cowsheds. Rowan was built into walls, and horseshoes hung up or discreetly buried under doorsteps. The common device of the foundation sacrifice is also found round the church. The Rev R. M. Heanley, watching some men building a churchyard wall in Hampshire, made a remark doubting its stability. 'Never fear,' replied the mason. 'He'll stand right enow, for I built your shadow into him yesterday when you wasn't looking.' Perhaps Mr Heanley's cloth gave added strength to the charm. *The Yorkshire Herald* for 31 May 1895 reported that when the tower of Darrington church near Pontefract, Yorkshire, was damaged in a gale, under the west side of the tower, in a bed of solid rock, was found the skeleton of a man, the west wall resting on his skull. It was thought to have been there 600 years. Three horse skulls, jaws uppermost, were found in 1877 in Elsdon church, Northumberland, in a cavity apparently specially built for them in the belfry, in a pagan pattern unmodified by Christian setting.[14] A witch bottle now in Cambridge Folk Museum came from the church tower of Swaffham Bulbeck, and during repairs at Nether Worton, Oxford-shire, 'footprints' cut from sheet lead (one dated 1659) were found in the church roof, an example of the not uncommon practice by work-men of scratching shoes and foot shapes on lead roofs, probably for protective or identification reasons.[15] Perhaps the builder merely wished to leave his mark, as did the Berkshire glazier who left the inscription 'C. Parker glased this church 1784 and glad of the job' upon a window in West Hendred church.[16]

Removing stone from ecclesiastical buildings was unwise, and elderly people round Aylesbury remember the direful warnings of judgement given to those who boldly took stones from the ruined Quarrendon chapel for farm purposes in the nineteenth century. But alabaster tombs sometimes owe their mutilated state to a general belief that scrapings from them were healing ingredients for medicines, a belief perhaps combining magic with chemistry. Over the years old shepherds chipped many fragments from Sir John Chydioke's tomb at Christchurch, for use in sheep nostrums.

Churchyards have always been places of presence and mystery, awe-inspiring enough to give authority to divinations practised and bargains struck within them, and often haunted. Typical of the many ec-clesiastical ghosts is Old Tanner, an amiable apparition in knee-breeches, who walks the churchyard at Hampstead Norris. A turf cut from a ghost's grave and laid under the altar for four days would effectively put an unwelcome phantom to rest. To horsewhip its grave was also helpful and the Rev Thomas Flavel, a formidable Cornish ghost-layer, never failed to take both prayer-book and whip when about his work. It is still felt to be unlucky to walk over or disturb a grave, perhaps the reason for the strenuous opposition often offered by parishioners to plans to level churchyards and rearrange gravestones for ease of maintenance, and for the reverence shown for churchyards by non-believers.

A new churchyard was full of menace and sometimes a dog was quietly selected for the doubtful honour of first burial within it, for the devil lays claim to the first corpse interred. A Somerset parson felt that one first burial had gone off unexpectedly smoothly until he noticed the absence from the neighbourhood of a large black dog, which would now 'keep the Old 'Un out'. The last to be buried in a churchyard became the 'watcher' until relieved by another. Sometimes two funerals might meet and it was not unheard of for the parties to gallop to be the one to reach the churchyard first and thus save the corpse in their care from this unpleasant office. Fights might break out, or attempts be made to hold rival mourners back. The last corpse to be buried in a churchyard before its closing was particularly unlucky, condemned to eternal watching, unless he were buried upside-down. The north side of the church—the 'devil's' or 'dog's side' —was shunned for burials and thought only fit for suicides, unbaptised children or tramps, who would walk in any case unless an animal were buried beneath them. While it is obviously difficult to discover how far this pagan lore is still regarded, Miss Tongue's Somerset findings during this century suggest that it is far from forgotten.

Milk from cows (often the parson's) kept in the churchyard, had healing virtue. (Some parsons went further and grew crops there: a visiting archdeacon said reprovingly to one vicar: 'Let me not see turnips when I come next time.' 'Certainly not!' said the unregenerate offender, practising the rotation of crops in unusual circumstances. 'It will be barley next year.') To destroy a churchyard yew was very ill-judged and William Coles told of a seventeenth-century clergyman who did this to his regret. He 'seeing some boyes breaking boughs from the yew-tree in the churchyard, thought himself much injured. To prevent like trespasses he sent one presently to cut down the tree, and to bring it into his backyard.' Two of the cows fed upon the leaves and died within a few hours, and the clergyman was thought well rewarded.[17] Magic wands from churchyard yew are specially potent: a Shropshire maker of wands, in a personal letter to the writer in 1970, noted: 'I have been very satisfied indeed with the magic I have had out of my own wand. It has simply crackled with magic . . .' Elderly Cambridgeshire folk feared cypresses in churchyards, saying that the spirits of the dead sheltered under them in bad weather.

Up to about 1840 it was the pleasant custom at Farndon, Cheshire, to dress graves with neatly arranged flowers and rushes on Whit-Monday and 'flowering the graves' was a widespread Easter custom. At Clyro in 1870, Parson Kilvert saw crowds coming to the church-yard with baskets of flowers for the Easter dressing, some carrying knives to cut holes in the turf to hold sprigs of blossom. Roses were often planted on graves: red roses spoke of the goodness of the deceased and white marked a virgin's grave. (The less popular might receive nettles or thistles.) John Aubrey noticed rose trees on graves at Ockley, Surrey, planted by the survivors of pairs of lovers, and this usage was not confined to England, for Miss Myrtle Bennett, a native of Waubaushene, Ontario, speaking in 1972 of its recently restored pioneer graveyard, unused for nearly one hundred years, said that it was particularly noted for the beauty of the roses planted on the graves by bereaved relatives.[18]

7

Country Cures and Remedies

Country cures and remedies either belong to the magico-religious, irrational group, or to those based on rational and valid folk-knowledge of plants and natural substances, probably largely acquired through fortuitous accident—and frequently administered with a strengthening charm. Dr Withering, for example, a practitioner who died in 1799, found a Shropshire wisewoman giving her patients a herb tea which included foxglove—containing digitalis, still a useful drug in the treatment of heart disease. Cures sometimes gained status in the clarifying light of science, but in general magic led the way. Dr David Speller comments:

> There is little in these bizarre and entertaining 'cures' that can have any basis in therapeutics. The foxglove story is one of the few instances where a country remedy has proved to contain an active pharmacological substance. Most of them are to be regarded as superstitious and magical, with success by the patient's belief, or by chance, or not at all. Many seem to be based on the most naïve sympathetic magic; lung-like lichen is used for lung disorders; the firecharm of the houseleek for burns, and so on. Most of all I see conditions notorious for spontaneous remission, or for varying severity; warts usually disappear, charmed or not, as immunity to the virus develops; malaria may burn itself out and in any case ague is followed cyclically by a sweating phase and then relief; epilepsy is variable even in severe cases; childhood hernias may resolve spontaneously. These diseases lend themselves to magical cures and charming, as failures and relapses can be put down to inability to obey all the complex and difficult conditions of the cure.[1]

Curative charms are often associated with unpleasant substances such as urine, lice, adders, spittle or stable air, and similarly, Dr Speller notes, it was customary until recent years to use such unpalatable flavourings as *asafoetida* in medicines to persuade the patient that they were doing him good. The comforting transference of disease to an animal, tree or other person, or the use of counter-irritants (such as gum-scratching for toothache), frequently appear in cures. Before science dealt with disease, hope and desire, emotions of intensity, were the most efficacious elements in cures, and old charmers knew, as Dr Jorden pointed out in 1603, that '. . . the confidence of the patient in the meanes used is oftentimes more available to cure diseases than all other remedies whatsoever.'[2]

Perhaps the secret of their apparent success was a stimulation of the patient's own healing mechanisms, a reinforcement of his host resistance to further attacks; he was invited to participate in his own cure, using a doctrine familiar to contemporary medicine, particularly in the treatment of mental illness. Such remedies made success a possibility for almost anyone provided he knew the method, for the power rested in ritual and detail, not (with comparatively rare exceptions) in the substances used, or in the charmer's own personality, and a great field of reassuring self-help home medicine was thus opened to the credulous and painstaking.

Even today old remedies have followers. Country doctors find shadows of ancient cures used alongside prescribed treatment, and while their total rejection and redundancy were accelerated by the advances of nineteenth-century medicine—the germ theory of disease, scientific nursing, X-rays, anaesthesia, asepsis—and later by the establishment of the National Health Service, it may be many years yet before it is completed, although in general the heyday of the folkcure had passed by 1914.

Healing substances included sacramental bread and wine, or bread baked on Good Friday or Christmas Day and crumbled into nostrums. 'Thank goodness,' said a Worcestershire farmer when it rained on Ascension Day in 1870. 'My old woman will be able to get some holy water.' For water caught 'straight from heaven' in a clean vessel on that day was an excellent remedy for cuts and sore eyes;[3] water caught from church roofs or from springs and wells of holy reputation was keenly sought after.

Onions are still said to absorb infections. During a nineteenth-century smallpox epidemic at Stockton Heath, Cheshire, a peeled onion hung over the post-office door; no one in the house caught the disease and when the onion was taken down it was found to be blackened and pitted, for 'the smallpox had flown straight to it' said the village.[4] A Frostburg, Maryland, woman remembered that if a stranger appeared at the farm, her mother insisted on throwing away any cut onions in the house, believing that they would have absorbed infections brought by him.[5] In an ingenious exercise of the doctrine of transference in the mid-nineteenth century, an old Huntingdonshire woman opened her windows during the evening to encourage gnats to enter a smallpox patient's room, later shooing the insects out to carry the disease away with them.[6]

In the New Forest, holed stones made potent by exposure to the rays of the full moon for three consecutive nights are worn by the sick. The seventh son of a seventh son is widely thought to have healing powers, and charmers and white witches (pow-wowers in the rural United States) continue active, especially in the West of England. Theo Brown of Chudleigh, writing in *Folklore*, 1970, told how, without making intensive enquiries, she came upon a number of charmers in Devon, working largely with non-herbal cures for complaints such as warts (at whose cure they are outstandingly successful), bleeding, burns, ringworm, sprains, snakebite and chilblains. Secrecy surrounds their work, which must not be done for gain, and while men or women may be charmers, the gift must be passed contra-sexually, man to woman or woman to man; charmers often receive their powers and word-charms from old persons anxious to pass their skills to a worthy successor. Theo Brown's findings are confirmed by those of Ruth E. St Leger-Gordon, which she discusses in *The Witch-craft and Folklore of Dartmoor*. Many charmers speak of the fatigue which follows the intense concentration on a patient vital to success.

The ring finger is healing but the forefinger—or 'poison finger'— must never be used to apply ointments. Spittle is therapeutic and is still applied to birthmarks and ringworm. Dr Speller comments:

'Spittle contains many bacteria, a teeming normal flora, an ecosystem. In the mouth it certainly helps to keep pathogens at bay. It also contains antibodies. It is impossible to rule out a healing role by these or other mechanisms, but it seems very unlikely. Probably it was merely a readily available secretion, like urine.'

Until the nineteenth century fevers were an ill-classified group. Ague or malarial fever, common in poorly-drained districts was wryly nicknamed 'the bailiff of the marshes' or 'Old Johnny'. In one counter-charm, horseshoes were nailed up by the charmer's left hand, to the words:

> Father, Son and Holy Ghost,
> Nail the Devil to the post,
> Thrice I smit with Holy Crook.
> With this mell I thrice do knock,
> One for God, one for Wod and one for Lok.

When, during an epidemic of 1857–8, the Rev R. M. Heanley took a patient the orthodox remedy of quinine, this was quickly rejected by the patient's grandmother, in charge of the sickroom; she preferred her own charm, saying 'When the Old 'Un comes to shak him he wean't nivver git past you . . .' pointing to three horseshoes nailed up with the hammer lying across them. Heanley was distressed by the rhyme's confusion of Christian and pagan *personae*, for Wod and Loki are Norse deities.[7] A farmer's wife near Aylesbury recommended marking a white chalk-mark round an iron kettle which was then put on the fire. As the mark burned away so would the disease magically disappear. An old Kentish woman believed that she had caught ague from a ribbon tied to her parents' gate by a sufferer anxious to abandon the disease, and sometimes a lock of the feverish patient's hair was nailed to, and it was hoped absorbed by, the sympathetically trembling aspen tree. Arthur Randell's parents swore by a pinch of dried and powdered mole's body added to a glass of gin on nine consecutive mornings, and the Ivinghoe schoolmaster was cured by taking, very hot, a pint of old beer and honey[8]—remedies which none could doubt were entirely effective.

The creamy juice of the houseleek, a charm against housefires, was appositely a soothing lotion for burns or inflamed insect bites. An Oxfordshire burn cure shows some elements of modern first-aid treatment giving relief and improved prognosis, for after the inner rind of the elder mixed with butter has been applied to the injury, the bandaged limb is plunged into cold water. A common West Country charm (with minor variations), is:

> Three Angels came from North, East and West,
> One brought fire, another brought frost,
> And the third brought the Holy Ghost.
> So out fire and in frost.
> In the name of the Father, Son and Holy Ghost.

West Country charmers often 'bless' for injuries such as burns. Ruth E. St Leger-Gordon tells of an encounter at a village meeting about 1958 with a woman who rolled up her sleeve to display a great scald mark from wrist to elbow, the result, she said, of an accident two days before. The only treatment needed had been for her to pass her hand over the injury and to recite a form of this charm, for she had the gift of 'blessing for burns'.[9]

Epilepsy, still a feared condition and once thought to be caused by evil-wishing, was cured with silver, powerful against enchantment. Patients collected nine pieces of silver and nine three-halfpennies from nine bachelors (if the patient were a girl) or spinsters (if a man); the silver was made into a ring to be worn by the patient and the coins presented to the maker. In 1830 a Suffolk man noticed a saucer full of silver scraps on the counter of a gunsmith's shop and was told that they had been left over from such a ring-making, although a more cynical Norfolk smith observed that he always kept a supply of readymade rings by him, and did not bother to make them from the proffered metal.[10]

Rheumatism, arthritis and similar complaints particularly afflicted agricultural workers living in damp, ill-heated cottages. Fenmen believed that an eelskin garter (from a symbolically lithe fish, as supple as the patient would wish to be) tied below the knee prevented rheumatism from rising higher, and elsewhere in both England and North

America a snakeskin was similarly used, as well as against cramp. A stolen dried potato or a cross-shaped elder bud (from a churchyard tree) in the pocket are well-tried remedies, and beekeepers attribute their freedom from rheumatism to the stings they receive. An old Dorset woman boasted that she had been confirmed several times by the bishop to relieve the pain of her joints.[11] Beating with a holly spray was advised in Somerset as recently as 1956, and Arthur Randell advocates the Fenland remedy of the dried front feet of a mole in the pocket nearest the affected limb. When the head of a contracting firm working in the Norfolk Fens near Mr Randell's home about 1965 complained of his 'screws', he was given four feet and returned within a week full of praise for the remedy. Since then Mr Randell has received a number of requests for moles' feet and testimonials as to their beneficial effects.[12] On Exmoor, where sciatica was graphically called 'boneshave', the patient was advised to lie upon the bank of a south-running stream with a straight stick between him and the water and to chant these words:

> Boneshave right, boneshave straight,
> As the water runs by the stave, good for boneshave.

William Ellis prescribed a *red* rag soaked in verjuice and tied overnight round the sprained wrists suffered by harvestmen each year before they became accustomed to the action of the scythe. Sometimes the soothing lotion was a mixture of urine and salt.[13] In Dorset, every second June until 1918, Bryanston bruise ointment was made of rosemary, sage, lavender, camomile, balm, betony, southernwood, red rosebuds and thistles, stirred into hogs' lard. Comfrey ('boneset' or 'knitbone') still has a place in the pharmacopoeia as a vulnerary. Earlier the glutinous root was grated for a plaster which set as hard as wood over a fracture, and it still lingers in many gardens; the writer noticed a thick border of comfrey round the farmyard at Manor Farm, Weston Turville in 1966.

The lichen 'brighten' and the flowers of eyebright and birdseye are ingredients for an eye lotion based upon sympathetic magic. For the childhood complaint of thrush, still quite common, three rushes, chosen because the words suggest the name of the disease, were drawn through the patient's mouth and then thrown into running water which carried the disease away. The vicar of Tormohun, Devon, reported about 1850 that one of his parishioners had ingeniously recited the eighth psalm, with the words 'out of the mouths of babes . . .', three times, three days running, to relieve her child's thrush. Water from a blacksmith's 'bosh' or cooling trough, linked with powerful iron and smith, was a healing drink for thrush patients and was also used in the treatment of ringworm, an ideal subject for charming since it varies greatly with season and skin dampness. In another connection George Ewart Evans tells of an inquisitive Suffolk farmer who, when the smith's back was turned, took a sample of bosh water; analysis revealed no appreciable amount of any substance other than iron rust, seeming to belie the water's high curative reputation.[14] A reducing charm for tetter, which appears to have included ringworm, impetigo and other skin diseases, was:

> Tetter, tetter, thou hast nine brothers,
> God bless the flesh and preserve the bone.
> Perish thou tetter and be thou gone!
> In the name of the Father . . .

recited down to 'thou hast no brothers', for the cure. A woman at Radley, Berkshire, allowed a village dog to lick her child's eczema sores, claiming biblical authority for this treatment in the story of Lazarus, and a Dorset gamekeeper called his dog 'Moreover' explaining 'Why, zur, its a real good Bible name for a dog. Ain't we told that "Moreover, the dog licked his sores." '[15]

Cambridgeshire mothers treating coughs and colds applied to the patient's chest a heart-shaped piece of brown paper (the shape was essential) over goosegrease, and Dorothy Hartley remembers being asked to hold the ladder for an old woman to climb up into a Leicestershire bell-chamber to fetch 'churchbell-grease' as an embrocation for her grandson's chest.[16] A small hot boiled onion is still sometimes pushed into an aching ear to relieve pain—both Miss Trump and Mrs Edwards remember this remedy.[17]

The bite of the adder, England's only poisonous snake, 'is rarely fatal in man, producing unpleasant symptoms only, from which recovery is the general rule—an ideal disease for a magical cure.'[18] A farmer at Sithney, Cornwall, was found about 1880 to be giving the victim of an adder-bite milk in which a 'serpent stone' or milpreene had been boiled. This naturally holed stone was popularly said to be formed by the hardened spittle of adders, who at certain times formed themselves into a living ball upon a hazel branch.[19] Two pieces of hazel wood were sometimes laid across the wound to the reducing rhyme:

> Underneath this hazelin mote,
> There's a bragotty worm with a speckled throat.
> Nine double is he:
> And from eight double to seven double,
> And from seven double to six double . . .

until the inflammation vanished. 'Blessing for sting' is found in Devon. West Country remedies for adder-bite were adapted by settlers in the United States for the far more dangerous bite of the rattlesnake and, as in England the snake's death was a requirement for cure, so in North America an offending rattlesnake was immediately killed and its flesh laid upon the bite. In Devon an adder-bite wound was pushed into the body of a freshly-killed chicken and in the United States the same cure (using as many as twelve chickens if necessary) was used to absorb rattlesnake poison, which would turn the chicken-flesh green.[20] Drawing its strength from the adder's sinister reputation, adder-fat was used for disorders from toothache to rheumatism; an adderskin hatband cured headaches and the skin or 'peal' drew thorns and needles from flesh as if by magic. In a carter's notebook of 1853, is a recipe for an ointment of peal, chickweed, primroses, wild celery root, resin and linseed, mixed with beeswax and hog's lard, for galls of all kinds, for bee and bot stings, for infected wounds and for growing hair, as well as for a bite from the snake itself. In one Sussex village an old man called 'Adder-fat Jack' hung the dead snakes on a fence in the sun, and collected their melted fat, which he sold profitably at sixpence a pot.[21]

Measles and whooping-cough were feared diseases of childhood. Measles had, from 1880–90, a mortality rate of 20 per 1,000 cases. Both diseases appear to have been more severe than they are today and in the absence of antibiotics, the secondary pneumonia, the usual cause of death, was untreatable. Charms and prophylactics abounded. In the late nineteenth century a Yorkshire farmer took his two children to the seaside to ride up and down nine times on donkeys, facing the animals' tails, and whether by chance or not the family escaped a local measles epidemic. The hairs from the dark 'cross' on a donkey's back, with holy associations, were chopped and given on bread and butter to a whooping-cough patient. In Sussex, children were taken on a donkey to a chosen place three times, three days running, and in one instance the parson's wife (who should have disapproved of so explicitly a pagan ritual) not only supplied the donkey, but made the bags in which its hairs were hung round the children's necks to reinforce the charm.

Riding a piebald horse was therapeutic, or its rider might be asked for advice, which must be followed to the letter. One kindly owner of a piebald always recommended sweets for the sick child and another 'patience and water gruel'. 'I well remember my mother giving me roasted mouse when I had whooping-cough about 1936,' said an Oxfordshire dairyman recently with a retrospective shudder, and William Edwards recalled the same cure with horror and could still 'cag' over it seventy years later. In Devon the sheep's 'yoke', the oily odour which occasionally made shearers sick, cured a whooping-cough patient, writes Miss Trump: 'A child so suffering would be lain on the grass from which a sheep had just risen, or a father would carry his child into the sheep market where the sheep were packed together and the heat of them would pervade the atmosphere'. Elsewhere children were passed three times, three mornings running before sunrise, over and under an arched briar or wild-rose shoot, to the words:

> Under the briar and over the briar,
> I wish to leave the chincough here,

and if bread and butter were left under the bush an animal taking it would absorb the disease. In Maryland the food was handed to the patient by a woman who had not changed her name by marriage, and, said old charmers, 'there will be no more "whoop" to that cough'. In Cheshire plain currant-cake was correct and in all cases no thanks were offered or expected for the food, or the charm would fail.[22] Sometimes at the end of the procedure the briar was made into a cross for the patient to wear. In Shropshire children afflicted with the complaint drank from ivywood cups, and one man made a useful living turning them, in wood from his brother's plantations, cut at the correct hour of night and moon's phase. But, reported an informant, by about 1850 these important requirements had unfortunately been forgotten.[23]

A common charm based, like the briar ritual, on the doctrine of symbolic rebirth in a state of wholeness, dealt with childhood hernia. An ash, willow, holly or hazel tree was split for part of its length, the two halves forced apart and the naked child pushed through the aperture, often on a Sunday before sunrise and in an east to west direction. The tree was then nailed or bound up and as the cut healed so would the hernia improve. Squire Leveson Gower of Titsey, Surrey, was walking with an old labourer in 1885 when they passed a holly tree at the roadside. 'I never go by that tree,' said the man 'without thinking of "Nurtey" being passed naked through it, sixty years ago. You can see the mark on the bark now.' The ruptured 'Nurtey', John Wolf of Limpsfield, lived to adulthood.[24] The charm is still a part of rural lore, and Miss Ruth Tongue writes that she saw a split ash in the Horner Valley, Somerset, about 1948, although she was sworn to secrecy as to its whereabouts. Woodmen were quite accustomed to finding nails in ash trees left from the rough cobbling which followed the charm's enactment.

Tuberculosis, and chest diseases in general, were common in farming communities, due to such factors as poor nutrition, overcrowding and exposure to dust; effective treatment of tuberculosis with streptomycin only began in the late 1940s. Earlier, an emulsion of snails dissolved in salt was taken with cream and sugar, or the patient made to sleep over the cowhouse to inhale its pungent, ammoniac odours. 'Hetherd-broth' of adder-flesh and chicken was taken in Lincolnshire, and Hampshire sufferers, wrote John Wise in *The New Forest* (1862), asked at the chemist's shop for a 'pennyworth of lungs of oak', the lichen *Sticta pulmonaria*, found on the sturdy oak trees of the forest. The host's strength and the lichen's lung-like form were components of this cure. In another remedy, even more clearly involving imitative magic, the lungs of a healthy sheep were bound to the patient's feet, a remedy found in use in Wales about forty years ago by at least one startled doctor.

Blacksmiths, the most powerful and respected members of the old rural community, were often credited with the power to arrest bleeding. When a Cornish man fell off a roof and, bleeding profusely, was hurried to the doctor, the smith ran out as the party passed the forge, ordered the rough bandage to be removed, and passed his hands over the cut, stopping the bleeding immediately. When the nose of a girl visitor at the Forest Inn, Hexworthy, on Dartmoor, began to bleed uncontrollably, the landlord's wife, a noted charmer, called Jack Warne, of Postbridge (who died in 1956 and who recalled the incident), into the next room and gave him a slip of paper with the words of a charm upon it; in this case a verse from Ezekiel (16:6), frequently used on such occasions:

And when I passed by thee, and saw thee polluted in thine own blood, I said unto thee when thou wast in thy blood, Live; yea, I said unto thee when thou wast in thy blood, Live.

This the girl was to read, but it was essential that the charm be administered by a person of the opposite sex, hence Mr Warne's participation. On this occasion at least the charm was apparently successful.[25] Powerful charmers can heal from a distance without seeing their patients,[26] and today the work may even be done by telephone.

Country housewives, however meticulous, took care to leave a few cobwebs undisturbed in the house for if bound over a cut they would stop bleeding—the finely divided surface of the web encouraged clotting. The practice is not yet forgotten. A curious wound doctrine, believed to prevent septicaemia, was that a scythe, knife or other implement, which had caused a wound, must be kept bright until healing was complete, and that if this precaution were neglected, infection would follow. A correspondent in Notes and Queries, 1876, wrote that a Shropshire clergyman's wife had injured her foot upon a nail in the garden and that the wound would not heal. The village 'doctress' consulted said that had the nail been thrust into a piece of fat bacon, healing would have been assured. In Adams County,

Illinois, updating the old doctrine, a slice of bacon is rubbed along a barbed-wire fence which has caused an injury. About fifty years ago, in another expression of this belief, a man in Brant County, Ontario, bitten during a pig-killing, took care to grease the pig's teeth carefully so that his wound might heal. In Tennessee a nail which had injured a child was at once greased and hammered into the east side of a sycamore tree, again to forestall infection. Richard Blakeborough, writing of Yorkshire in 1898, remembered that within the past ten years when a lad was injured in a ploughing accident, work was stopped at once and the coulter quickly removed from the plough and sent to the blacksmith, with instructions to clean and polish the parts to which blood adhered. Each time the wound was dressed during the boy's recovery, burnishing was repeated.[27]

Counter-irritants and transferred pain appeared in toothache cures; typically a nail or splinter of wood, often from a lightning-struck tree, was used to scratch the gum to bleeding point and then hammered into the tree to leave the pain behind. Very common, too, was the charm:

> Peter sat weeping on a marble stone
> Jesus came and said,
> 'What aileth thou, O Peter?'
> He answereth and said,
> 'My Lord and my God'.
> He that can say this, and believeth it for My Sake
> Never no more shall have the toothache.

Jaundice gives the patient's skin a yellowish cast and the disease was thus treated with the yellow flowers of gorse, saffron, barberry or jaundice tree, amber, a yellow rag, gold coin, or with elder milk. In Suffolk a bottle of the patient's urine was dropped uncorked into a stream and as the water blended with the urine and cleared it, so would the jaundice disappear.[28] In a less agreeable ritual, perhaps intended to cure by shock, the patient must eat nine lice on bread and butter. 'I am bound to state,' wrote a Dorset observer about 1850, 'for the credit of the parish, that the animalcules were somewhat difficult of attainment; but that, after having been duly collected by the indefatigable labours of the village doctress, they were administered with the most perfect success.'[29] The lice, it was claimed, would go directly to the liver to clear the disease. In another piece of sympathetic magic, parsley piert or breakstone, which favoured stony ground, was used against kidney stones.

Boils were formerly far more common than they are today and Mrs Baker writes of a Rye schoolfriend, the daughter of a fisherman, about 1905: 'She was pleased to show me her hand, padded with petals of the madonna lily, which she said had been pickled in brandy. It was a commonly-used remedy. The rough side of the petals was used for drawing and the smooth side for healing.'

Allusions in old cures to hydrophobia can hardly indicate the true rabies, which is still almost invariably fatal and exceedingly rare in England. But the cures were perhaps intended to alleviate the pain, fever and shock which might follow the bite of a dog. In one magical remedy the dog's hair was chopped and mixed with the patient's food, the origin of the phrase 'the hair of the dog that bit you'. *The Pall Mall Gazette* for 12 October 1866 reported a strange variant which came to light at an inquest. A child had been bitten by a dog at Bradwell, Buckinghamshire, about two weeks earlier; the animal was killed and its body tossed into the canal. An old woman then advised that it should be dragged out and its liver given to the sick child to eat; this was done, and although the patient ate the liver with keen appetite, he died nevertheless.

Fertility was an abiding preoccupation of the rural community and as highly prized in farmhouse as in farmyard. The stone from a capon's gizzard made a man an attractive and virile lover, but most potent of all fertility devices was the mandrake, for which bryony or 'big-root' was often mistaken or substituted. This anthropomorphic, bifurcated root was said to prevent sterility in both man and beast, but its gathering was hazardous; the shriek of the plant as it was pulled from the ground caused madness. Prudent collectors tied a hungry dog to the mandrake and placed a dish of meat nearby, so that the leaping animal would suffer the consequences of the plant's cry. Once out of the ground the plant was perfectly safe to handle. 'Old Fitch', a Victorian chemist at Littleport, Cambridgeshire, paid sixpence a pound for mandrake roots to be made into an aphrodisiac guaranteed to make old men strong and to put new life into weary women at the price of one shilling a bottle.[30] The mandrake's reputation is far from forgotten and it may still find a place in country pockets, round country bed-posts and in the stable. In East Anglia, in a more obvious charm, a childless couple were advised to sleep with the dried testicle of a castrated stallion under the pillow. Sage juice drunk four days after menstruation will have a similarly stimulating effect; tansy flourishes where rabbits abound, therefore tansy juice induces conception; parsley and sage do best where the wife rules, and a thriving parsley patch or sage-bush means only girls will be born to the family.[31]

Mineral deficiencies in the water supplies of some districts caused goitres (enlargements of the thyroid gland), given local names such as Derbyshire neck. In Sussex, a grass snake was held by head and tail and passed nine times over the affected part, then corked up alive in a bottle and buried. As it decomposed so would the swelling diminish. Hair from a grey stallion's tail, a symbolic source of strength, made a therapeutic necklace, but the groom must not be told the purpose for which it was needed. 'The plaited necklace,' wrote one observer, 'fastened in front with a neat gold snap, makes a rather attractive ornament amongst farmers' daughters'.[32] A woman at Cuddesdon, Oxfordshire, mentioning another popular remedy for the complaint, told a visitor about 1845 that she would have liked to treat her goitre with the 'dead stroke'—a touch of the hand of a dead man; her father had cured his goitre in this way and she was waiting a suitable opportunity to do likewise.[33]

Wart-lore is as active and mysterious today as at any time in its long life. In a common charm, notches are cut in an elder stick to corres-pond with the number of warts to be cured. The stick is buried and as it decays so will the warts disappear. Mrs Cecil Atkins told the writer in 1969 that this cure had been used with perfect success at Waddesdon within the last few years. There are many variants as to materials: a stone, beanpod, apple, green sloe, or slice of bacon or meat, have all been recommended and may be buried or wrapped in an inviting small parcel which is dropped at a crossroads. Whoever picks it up will acquire the warts. Greater celandine juice and, in North America, milkweed juice, are charm lotions which cause gratifying colour changes. Charmers must be reticent and Mrs Cecil Newcomb of Walton, Nova Scotia, told the writer in 1971: 'I was very irate, as a child, when an aunt and my elder sister whispered together. My aunt was curing my sister's warts and wouldn't tell me their secret.'

Mr D. St Leger-Gordon told the story in *Devonshire*, 1953, of an East Devon farmer, badly afflicted with warts on his hands for many years who happened to visit a Tiverton ironmonger's shop. The proprietor happened to notice his disfigured hands and declared that, although he could not account for the gift, he had the power to cure them; he rubbed the farmer's hands within his own, and the patient reported that the warts were itching by the time he reached home and within a week had vanished, never to return. A charmer who lived near Ottery St Mary and who died, aged eighty-seven, shortly before 1965, was skilled at 'shaking hands for warts', and indeed for a long while attended each Friday market at Exeter in his charmer's capacity, and to give advice on such problems as bewitchment.[34]

In Leicestershire, invoking another form of transference, the patient visited an ash tree and each wart was carefully pricked with a new pin, which was then driven into the tree's bark to the words:

Ashen tree, ashen tree,
Pray buy these warts of me.

And Arthur Randell well remembers his father offering to buy Fenland sufferers' warts for a halfpenny, with complete success. There are many charms, but whatever their nature and secret, wart-healing remains one of the most baffling and lively expressions of folk-medicine today, so effective that open-minded general practitioners, conscious of conventional remedies' frequent lack of success with stubborn warts, sometimes refer sufferers to local charmers.

Notes and References

(Each book included is described fully in the Bibliography and in its first References entry.)

Introduction
(pages 9–13)

1 Gibbs, J. Arthur, *Cotswold Countryman*, 1898 (as *A Cotswold Village*, reprinted 1967), 170
2 Trump, A. M., 'Things My Grandmother Told Me' (manuscript, unpublished)
3 Hone, W., *Year Book*, 1864, 477
4 Fairfax-Blakeborough, J. and R., *The Spirit of Yorkshire*, 1954, 178. Major J. Fairfax-Blakeborough is an authority on Yorkshire life. The writings of his father, Richard Blakeborough, include *Wit, Character, Folk Lore and Customs of the North Riding of Yorkshire*, 1898, and the dialect classic *T' Hunt o' Yatton Brig*, 1899
5 Harman, H., *Buckinghamshire Dialect*, 1929 (reprinted Wakefield 1970), 99
6 Rose, Walter, *Good Neighbours*, 1943, 1. The Rose family had long connections with farming and building in Haddenham, Buckinghamshire
7 Drabble, Phil, 'Staffordshire Unvisited', *The Countryman*, Autumn 1966, 20–8

1: On the Farm: Fields and Fertility
(pages 15–35)

1 *Daily Graphic*, 1 January 1898, 3; *Notes and Queries*, 1859, ser 2, v 8, 488
2 Fletcher, H. L. V., *Herefordshire*, 1948, 45–6, quoting Parry, Richard, *The History of Kington*, 1845

Notes and References

3 Kilvert, F., *Diary* 1870-9, ed William Plomer, 1944, 321-2. Francis Kilvert, born 1840, was successively curate of Langley Burrell, Wiltshire, Clyro, St Harmon's, Radnorshire, and vicar of Bredwardine, Herefordshire

4 Morris, L. E., Ruislip, Middlesex. Personal letter 23 January 1972

5 Cameron, Kenneth, *English Place-Names*, 1961, 205, 209

6 *Blundell's Diary and Letter Book 1702-28*, ed M. Blundell, Liverpool 1952, 138

7 Martin, E. W., *The Secret People*, 1954, 69-70

8 *Halifax Chronicle-Herald*, 4 October 1971, 10; *The Countryman*, Autumn 1972, 124-31

9 *Transactions Devonshire Association*, Plymouth, 1884, v 16, 122. Letter from J. M. Hawker, 5 October 1883. The reading of Genesis commences on Septuagesima Sunday

10 Hone, *Year Book*, 1864, 798

11 William Cobbett (1763-1835) scared birds from turnip seed and peas at so early an age that climbing gates and stiles was a problem

12 Mrs E. Fields, Economy, Nova Scotia. Personal letter 1 October 1971

13 The poisonous seeds of *Lychnis githago*, the corncockle, if ground with wheat may cause sickness and vertigo

14 Rose, Walter, *Good Neighbours*, 1943, 23

15 Cullum, J., *The History and Antiquities of Hawstead in the County of Suffolk*, 1784, 87

16 Marshall, Sybil, *Fenland Chronicle*, Cambridge 1967, 119. Recollections of William Henry Edwards (1860-1940), a Huntingdonshire fenman, and of his wife, Kate Mary, collected and edited by their daughter

17 Blythe, R., *Akenfield: Portrait of an English Village*, 1969, 55

18 Lethaby, W. R., *Home and Country Arts*, 1924, 98

19 Herrick, Robert, *Poems*, ed L. C. Martin, Oxford 1965, 101. Herrick (1630-74), vicar of Dean Prior, Devon, professed to dislike country life, but was its close observer

20 Peate, Iorwerth C., 'Corn Ornaments', *Folklore*, Autumn 1971, 82, 177-84. Notable corn-dolly makers today include Emmie White of Northaw, Hertfordshire, author of *Making Corn Dollies*, Northaw 1971, and Angela Gibson, Stow-on-the-Wold, Gloucestershire

21 Lambeth, M., *A New Golden Dolly*, Fulbourn 1963, 52; Porter, Enid, *Cambridgeshire Customs and Folklore*, 1969, 123-4

22 Hone, W., *Every-Day Book*, 1827, 2, 1155

23 Hone, W., *The Table Book*, 1864, 705

24 Hughes, Anne, *The Diary of a Farmer's Wife 1796–1797*, 1964, 65–8. Anne's husband John was a Herefordshire farmer. She was twenty-four at the time of the *Diary*

25 Gibbs, J. Arthur, *Cotswold Countryman*, 1898 (as *A Cotswold Village* reprinted 1967), 33

26 Dacombe, Marianne R., ed, *Dorset Up Along and Down Along*, Dorchester 1951, 107. Arthur Randell is a present-day exponent of the broomstick dance. See *Sixty Years a Fenman*, 1966, plate 13

27 Williams, Alfred, *A Wiltshire Village*, 1912, 119–20

28 Major J. Fairfax-Blakeborough, Westerdale. Personal letter 31 March 1972. See also Fairfax-Blakeborough, J. and R., *The Spirit of Yorkshire*, 1954, 181–2

29 Thwaites, Neil R., 'Corn Dollies in East Yorkshire', *English Dance and Song*, 32 no 4, 128–9

2: On the Farm: Stock, Dairy and Orchard
(pages 36–57)

1 Meynell, Esther, *Sussex*, 1966, 217 quoting *West Sussex Gazette*, 1912

2 Beckett, Arthur, *The Spirit of the Downs*, 1909, 287–8; H. R. H. Harmer. Personal letter 28 July 1972; Stamp, L. Dudley, *Man and the Land*, 1955, 133: *Sussex Notes and Queries*, 1926, I, no 3, 70

3 Humphreys, A. L., *The History of Wellington*, 1889, 235. The 'ladder' is in the Pitt Rivers Museum, Oxford; Tongue, Ruth L., *Somerset Folklore*, 1965, 67

4 *Canadian Folk-Lore*, reprinted from *The Journal of American Folk-Lore*, 31, nos 119–20, Lancaster, Pennsylvania 1918, 40

5 Collins, William, *Ode on the Popular Superstitions of the Highlands of Scotland*, Edinburgh 1788, 10; Ramsay, Allan, *Poems*, Edinburgh 1720–2, 224

6 Farisees—a dialect word for fairy, derived from Gaelic fear-sidhean—fairy-men; Brand, John, *Observations on the Popular Antiquities of Great Britain*, 1849, v 2, 503

7 Mrs Olive Bedford, Gildersome, Yorkshire. Personal letter 6 February 1972

8 Pitt Rivers Museum, Oxford

Notes and References

9 St Leger-Gordon, Ruth E., *The Witchcraft and Folklore of Dartmoor*, 1965, reprinted Wakefield 1972, 160

10 Tyack, George S., *The Lore and Legend of the English Church*, 1899, 223

11 *The Times*, 7 September 1971, 11; see also Evans, George Ewart, *The Horse in the Furrow*, 1960, 238–71

12 Hankey, M., 'Gypsy Recipe', *The Countryman*, Winter 1967, 431

13 Arthur Randell. Personal letter 29 June 1972. See also *Sixty Years a Fenman*, 1966, 106–9

14 Wolseley, Viscountess, *The Countryman's Log-Book*, 1921, 297

15 Vince, John, *Discovering Carts and Wagons*, Tring 1970, 13–14

16 Benfield, Eric, *Dorset*, 1950, 123–4

17 Coles, William, *Adam in Eden*, 1657, 561

18 Beckett, Arthur, *The Spirit of the Downs*, 1909, 92–3

19 O'Neill, Hannah Cox, *Devonshire Idyls*, 1892, 177–81

20 Fairfax-Blakeborough, J. and R., *The Spirit of Yorkshire*, 1954, 160

21 Clare, John, *The Shepherd's Calendar*, Oxford 1964, 67–8

22 Manners, J. E., 'The Language of Sheep Bells', *Country Life*, 8 April 1971, 839

23 Boyd, A. W., *The Country Diary of a Cheshire Man*, 1946, 46

24 St Leger-Gordon, D., *Devonshire*, 1950, 273

25 *The Times*, 8 December 1924, 32

26 Whistler, L., *The English Festivals*, 1947, 79; Palmer, K. and Patten, R. W., 'Some Notes on Wassailling and Ashen Faggots in South and West Somerset', *Folklore*, 1971, 82 no 4, 281–91

27 *Cotswold Life*, March 1972, 52. Letter from Mrs D. D. Houlton, Burford

28 Ms Bernice Fuller, Traverse City Area Chamber of Trade. Personal letter 9 March 1972

29 *Notes and Queries*, 1870, ser 4, v 6, 130

30 Baïracli-Levy, J. de, *Wanderers in the New Forest*, 1958, 125–6

31 Hone, *Table Book*, 1864, 337–8. Wiggen or wicken are alternative names for rowan or mountain ash

32 Ady, Thomas, *A Candle in the Dark*, 1655, 58; Burne, Charlotte, *A Handbook of Folklore*, 1914, 67–8

33 Robinson, F. K. A., *A Glossary of Words Used in the Neighbourhood of Whitby*, 1876, 148

34 Aubrey, John, *Remaines of Gentilisme and Judaisme*, 1881 ed, 243

35 Bedell, E. W., *An Account of Hornsea in Holderness in the East-Riding of Yorkshire*, Hull 1848, 89

36 Turner, W. J., *Exmoor Village*, 1947, plate 10

37 Brown, Theo, 'Charming in Devon', *Folklore*, Spring 1970, 81, 43; *Transactions Devonshire Association*, 1963, 95, 98; Botkin, B. A., ed, *A Treasury of New England Folklore*, New York 1965, quoting Newell, W. W., 'Conjuring Rats', *Journal of American Folklore*, 1892, 4, xvi, Jan–Mar, 23–4; Boyd, A. W., *The Country Diary of a Cheshire Man*, 1946, 283

38 Pollard, P., Cornwall, nd, 18

39 Smith, W. L., *Pioneers of Old Ontario*, Toronto 1923, 176

40 Major J. Fairfax-Blakeborough. Personal letter 31 March 1972; Lambeth, M., *A New Golden Dolly*, Fulbourn 1963, 91–2

3: House and Garden Magic
(pages 58–88)

1 *Choice Notes from 'Notes and Queries': Folk Lore*, 1859, 129–30: Baïracli-Levy, J. de, *Wanderers in the New Forest*, 1958, 125–6

2 Rich, Louise Dickinson, *The Peninsula*, New York, Philadelphia 1958, 272; Creighton, Helen, *Bluenose Magic: Popular Beliefs and Superstitions in Nova Scotia*, Toronto 1968, 39, 167

3 Christopher D. Sansom, Kennel Moor, near Godalming. Personal letter 2 April 1973; White, Gilbert, *The Natural History and Antiquities of Selborne*, ed Frank Buckland, 1875, 10

4 *Dalesman*, 1970, 717; 1971, 627; Pollard, P., *Cornwall*, nd, 18

5 Dacombe, 116. Account from Mrs Carlton of Winterbourne Kingston, 1930

6 *Notes and Queries*, 1856, ser 2, v 1, 415; 1872, ser 4, v 9, 255

7 Mrs E. Lahey, curator, Lundy's Lane Historical Museum, Niagara Falls, Ontario. Personal letter 4 July 1972. The St David's shoe, now in the Lundy's Lane Museum, came from the house of Mr and Mrs Arnold Doyle. Miss J. M. Swann, assistant curator of Northampton Museum, published the results of her research to that date on this subject, with a list of finds, in 'Shoes Concealed in Buildings', *Journal no 6, Northampton Museum*, 1969. Finds since then, totalling 73 to June 1972, include in North America examples from Millgrove, Ontario (child's leg-boot, late nineteenth century); St Catherines, Ontario (boy's button boot, in the stair wall of a building completed January 1906); Welland, Ontario (child's lace boot cut at vamp, nineteenth century); the Abbs Valley example.

Notes and References

For the first time finds have been reported from Yorkshire and Scotland, suggesting that the practice may have been more widespread than earlier investigations revealed. Personal letters June 1972

8 Moore, John, *Man and Bird and Beast*, 1959, 200–1
9 Duncan S. Gray, Toronto. 6 July 1972. Oral report.
10 Pitt Rivers Museum, Oxford
11 Radford, E. and M. A., *Encyclopaedia of Superstitions*, ed and rev by Christina Hole, 1961, 268, quoting Hood, C. M., 'Scraps of English Folklore: North Norfolk', *Folk-Lore*, 1926, 37
12 Smith, George, *Six Pastorals*, 1770, 30
13 Patterson, George, 'Notes on the Folk-Lore of Newfoundland'. Paper read to the Boston branch, American Folklore Society, 17 January 1894
14 Porter, 391
15 Strangers' Hall Museum, Norwich has a 'feather-luck' in its collection
16 *Choice Notes*, 1859, 62
17 *Murray's Handbook for Berks, Bucks, and Oxfordshire*, 1882, 152
18 Fletcher, H. L. V., *Herefordshire*, 1948, 47–8
19 Mrs Cecil C. Newcomb, Walton, Nova Scotia. Personal letter 30 September 1971
20 F. Bennett, Production Manager, H. P. Bulmer Limited, Hereford. Personal letter 18 July 1972
21 Moore, John, *Man and Bird and Beast*, 1959, 168
22 Southey, Robert, *Letters from England*, ed Jack Simmons, 1951, 189
23 Bell, Vicars, *To Meet Mr Ellis*, 1956, 27–8. William Ellis (1700–58), the Hertfordshire farmer-writer of Little Gaddesden, wrote authoritatively, but visitors to Church Farm suggested that his farming theories were sounder than his practice
24 The baiver story was a favourite of the late Jack Uff of Waddesdon
25 Black puddings of pigs' blood, oatmeal, herbs, spices, eggs and milk were (and are) a favourite in the north of England. White puddings are a kind of cereal sausage. Rundell, Mrs, *A New System of Domestic Cookery* 1835, 64–6
26 See also *Folk-Lore*, Spring 1941, 52, 75. Letter from Rev Peter B. C. Binnell, Holland Fen, Lincoln; *Notes and Queries*, 1878, ser 5, v 10, 514
27 Christopher D. Sansom, Kennel Moor, near Godalming. Personal letter 18 March 1973
28 L. E. Morris, Ruislip. Personal letter 23 January 1972 reporting a conversation in a Bledlow public-house in the Chilterns in the late 1920s or early 1930s

29 Beresford, W., *Memorials of Old Staffordshire*, 1909, 92–3
30 *Choice Notes*, 71
31 Jackson, Ada, 'Bees are People', *The Countryman*, Autumn 1967, 188–93
32 Brand 2, 301 quoting *The Argus*, 13 September 1790
33 Christopher D. Sansom, Kennel Moor, near Godalming. Personal letter 18 March 1973
34 Mrs Alice Florence Smith, Patchway, Bristol. Personal letter 2 April 1973
35 Mrs E. E. Bowes, Burton Lazars, Leicestershire. Personal letter 5 March 1973
36 Mrs A. E. Monk, Sherborne, Dorset. Personal letter 30 March 1973
37 Miss Nancy J. Quayle, Bury, Pulborough, Sussex. Personal letter 28 February 1973
38 Cook, Doris C. ed, 'An Elizabethan Guernseyman's Manuscript Book of Gardening and Medical Secrets' in *The Channel Islands Annual Anthology 1972–1973*, Stevens-Cox, J. and G. eds, Guernsey 1972, 34. The manuscript, dated 1589, is of Thomas Andros, born 1571, a descendant of John Andrews of Northampton who settled in Guernsey about 1543
39 J. E. Ronald Griffiths, Toronto. Oral report 14 March 1973
40 Mrs Cranston Smallwood, Sene Park, Hythe, Kent. Personal letter 29 February 1973
41 Frank J. Taylor, Acock's Green, Birmingham. Personal letter 5 March 1973; W. Walton, Garton-on-the-Wolds, Yorkshire. Personal letter 27 May 1973; F. W. Baty, Longhope, Gloucestershire. Personal letter 18 May 1973; Evans, George Ewart, *The Pattern Under the Plough*, 1966, 45
42 Mead, Harry, 'The Great Gooseberry Contest', *In Britain*, August 1972, 26–7

4: Country Calendar
(pages 89–132)

1 Brand, 1877, 263, quoting Stevenson, T., *Twelve Moneths*, 1661
2 Brand, 1877, 275, quoting *Tusser Redivivus*, 1744
3 Blakeborough, 66–7
4 Hunt, R., *Cornish Customs and Superstitions*, Truro, nd, 14–15; Whitney, Annie Weston and Bullock, Caroline Canfield, *Folk-Lore of Maryland*, New York 1925, 128; Creighton, 134

Notes and References

5   Blakeborough, 68

6   Anspach, L. A., *History of the Island of Newfoundland*, 1819, 475

7   Albert Van Citters, The Empress Hotel, Victoria, British Columbia.
Personal letter 28 April 1972

8   Hughes, 114-15

9   *Notes and Queries*, 1883, ser 6, v 8, 482; 1892, ser 8, v 2, 506-7

10 Rose, 135

11 Wassail, from ME *wase hail*—'be fortunate'

12 Lamb, Elizabeth, 'Cornish Wassailling Today', *English Dance and Song*,
Winter 1971, 132-3; Baur, John, *Christmas on the American Frontier 1800–
1900*, Caldwell, Idaho 1961, 193-4

13 The Director, Royal Botanic Gardens, Kew. Personal letter 31 March
1972

14 Harland, John and Wilkinson, T. T., *Lancashire Folk-Lore*, 1867, 20

15 Hole, Christina, *Saints in Folklore*, New York 1965, 44-5, quoting *The
Times*, 14 January 1949

16 Lord, Priscilla Sawyer and Foley, Daniel J., *Easter Garland*, New York and
Philadelphia, 1963, 10

17 Tiddy, R. J. E., *The Mummers' Play*, Oxford 1923, reprinted Chicheley,
1972; Chambers, E. K., *The English Folk-Play*, 1933. For complete texts
or extracts of plays mentioned see: Welch, Charles E. Jr, 'O, Dem Golden
Slippers', *Journal of American Folklore*, 1966, 79, 523-36; Halpert, H. and
Story, G. M. eds, *Christmas Mumming in Newfoundland*, Toronto 1969;
Rose, Walter, *Good Neighbours*, 1943, 131-5; *The Berkshire Book; Com-
piled by the Berkshire Federation of Women's Institutes*, Reading 1951;
Uttley, Alison, *Buckinghamshire*, 1950, 404-9; Coffin, Tristram P. and
Cohen, Hennig eds, *Folklore in America*, New York 1966, 205-11; Long,
George, *The Folklore Calendar*, 1930, 223-31; Udal, J. S., *Dorsetshire
Folk-Lore*, 1922, reprinted Guernsey 1970

18 *Notes and Queries*, 1857, ser 2, v 3, 343

19 Baty, F. W., *The Forest of Dean*, 1952, 27; *Folk-Lore*, 1902, 13, 174

20 Addy, S. O., *Household Tales*, 1895, 103

21 Mathews, F. W., *Tales of the Blackdown Borderland*, 1923, 119

22 Jack Scarth, leader of the Goathland Plough Stots and Mrs Jean Williamson, Grosmont, Whitby. Personal letters July 1972

23 Marshall, 201

24 Hone, *Year Book*, 1864, 800

25 Glenn E. Gavin, Liberal Chamber of Commerce. Personal letter 23 May
1972

26 *Cheshire Village Memories: Being Extracts from Seventy-Four Scrapbooks of Local History Made by Members of the Women's Institutes,* Malpas 1969, 120

27 Morley, G., *Shakespeare's Greenwood,* 1900, 105

28 Lane, Margaret, *The Tale of Beatrix Potter,* 1946, 169; Danielli, Mary, 'Jollyboys, or Pace Eggers, in Westmorland', *Folk-Lore,* 1951, 62, 463-7

29 *Transactions of the Devonshire Association,* Plymouth 1876, 8, 57-8

30 *Kent and Sussex Courier,* 7 April 1972, 36

31 Tongue, 160

32 Hone, *Every-Day Book,* 1, 422-4

33 Harland, 233-4

34 Noake, John, *Notes and Queries for Worcestershire,* 1856, 212

35 Boyd, A. W., *The Country Diary of a Cheshire Man,* 1946, 289

36 Gibson, A. Craig, 'Ancient Customs of Cumberland', *Transactions of the Historical Society of Lancashire and Cheshire,* 1858, 10, 104

37 Chambers, R. ed, *The Book of Days,* 1862-4, 1, 572, quoting Irving, Washington, *The Sketchbook of Geoffrey Crayon, Esq.,* 1820

38 Hardwick, Charles, *Traditions, Superstitions, and Folk-Lore (Chiefly Lancashire and the North of England),* Manchester 1872, 90-1

39 Foxworthy, Tony, 'West Country Customs', *English Dance and Song,* Spring 1971, 16-17; Gammon, Laura M. R., 'Chalgrove: A Sketch', *The Pelican,* February 1883, 7-8

40 Shepard, E. H., *Drawn from Memory,* 1957, 54-6

41 Hone, *Table Book,* 1864, 277

42 Hone, *Every-Day Book,* 2, 599-600; Porter 396-7, plate 77

43 Bazier or bear's-ear—auricula

44 Thompson, Flora, *Lark Rise to Candleford,* 1954, 217-25

45 Hone, *Every-Day Book,* 2, 792-4

46 Hone, *Every-Day Book,* 2, 707-9

47 Beckett, Arthur, *The Spirit of the Downs,* 1909, 292-7

48 *Sussex Archaeological Society Collections,* Lewes 1883, 33, 246

49 Gosse, P. H., 'Schooldays in Dorset 1818-1823', *Longmans Magazine,* 1889, 13, 517

50 Tongue, 166

51 Harman, 93-4

52 Morley, G., *Shakespeare's Greenwood,* 1900, 121-2

53 Eden, Sir Frederick, *Survey of the Condition of the Poor in the Famine of the Years 1795-1796,* 1797, 1, 32

54 Brand, 2, 455-6 quoting *Preston Guardian,* 1845

Notes and References

55 Baker, M. C., 'Memories of a Sussex Childhood 1894–1905', unpublished.
56 Williams, Keith, 'My Village Scene', *In Britain*, June 1972, 35–7
57 Oral report by Martha Chapman, 1910, collected by Mrs F. S. Chapman. Wright, Arthur R. and Lones, T. E., *British Calendar Customs: England*, 1940, 3, 178
58 Tongue, 172

5: From Cradle to Grave
(pages 133–54)

1 Williams, Keith, 'My Village Scene', *In Britain*, June 1972, 35–7
2 *Folk-Lore*, Spring 1941, 52, 75. Letter from the Rev Peter B. C. Binnell, Vicar of Holland Fen, Lincoln
3 Tongue, 65
4 Waldron, George, *A Description of the Isle of Man*, 1731, 128
5 Paterson, George, 'Notes on the Dialect of the People of Newfoundland', *Journal of American Folklore*, 1896, 9, 22
6 Green, Peter, *Kenneth Grahame 1859–1932: a Study of His Life, Work and Times*, 1959, 267
7 Davies, Joseph, 'Bundling', *The Countryman Book*, 1948, 194–6; Porter, 4
8 Tyack, 68
9 *Notes and Queries*, 1868, ser 4, v 2, 450
10 Blakeborough, 100–1
11 Baring-Gould, Sabine, *A Book of Folk-Lore*, nd, 257–8; Henderson, W., *Notes on the Folk-Lore of the Northern Counties of England and the Borders*, 1866, 23–4
12 Macaulay, 130
13 Woodford, Cecile, *Portrait of Sussex*, 1972, 205
14 Atkinson, J. C., *Forty Years in a Moorland Parish*, 1891, 210
15 Rose, 98
16 Duncan S. Gray, Toronto, 1972
17 Baring-Gould, Sabine, *Devonshire Characters and Strange Events*, 1908, 60; *Chambers' Book of Days*, 1, 487–8
18 *The Newbury Weekly Press*, 21 February 1963, 11
19 Skelton, Isabel, *The Backwoodswoman*, Toronto 1924, 252
20 Harland, 270; Nichols, J., *History and Antiquities of the County of Leicestershire*, 1811, 2, part 1, 357

21 Bosworth Smith, R., *Bird Life and Bird Lore*, 1905, 357; MacCulloch, E., *Guernsey Folklore*, 1903, 105

22 Macaulay, Aulay, *The History and Antiquities of Claybrook in the County of Leicester*, 1791, 131

23 Udal, J. S., *Dorsetshire Folk-Lore*, 1922, reprinted Guernsey 1970, 187

24 *Notes and Queries*, 1892, ser 8, v 1, 343

6: The Country Church
(pages 155–68)

1 Kilvert, 324–5

2 Wolseley, 229. Geneva—a gin made in Holland, also called Hollands

3 Macaulay, 93

4 Brand, 1877, 159

5 *Chambers' Book of Days*, 1, 506; Hone, *Year Book*, 1864, 552–3

6 Brand, 1849, 2, 375. The Duke of Devonshire's seat, Chatsworth, is a few miles from Buxton

7 Edwards, H., *A Collection of Old English Customs and Curious Bequests and Charities*, 1842, 34–5

8 *The Countryman*, Spring 1967, 203; Autumn 1966, 20

9 Tongue, 166–7

10 *Notes and Queries*, 1893, ser 8, v 3, 462–3; Savory, Arthur, *Grain and Chaff from an English Manor*, 1920, 94

11 *Cheshire Village Memories*, 63, 90

12 Boyd, A. W., *The Country Diary of a Cheshire Man*, 1946, 260

13 Cameron, Kenneth, *English Place-Names*, 1961, 210; Edwards, 208

14 Gomme, George Laurence, *Ethnology in Folklore*, 1892, 35–6; *Notes and Queries*, 1880, ser 6, v, 424

15 Alan Trump, Ledwell, Oxfordshire

16 *The Berkshire Book*, 149

17 Coles, William, *The Art of Simpling: An Introduction to the Knowledge and Gathering of Plants*, 1656, 59

18 *The Free Press* (Midland, Ontario), 28 July 1972, 1, 3

Notes and References

7: *Country Cures and Remedies*
(pages 169–83)

1 Dr David Speller (University of Bristol). Personal letter 20 June 1972
2 Jorden, Dr A., *A Briefe Discourse of a Disease Called the Suffocation of the Mother*, 1603, 24
3 Reiss, F. A., *The History of the Parish of Rock*, nd, 37
4 Boyd, A. W., *The Country Diary of a Cheshire Man*, 1946, 67
5 Whitney and Bullock, 58
6 *Notes and Queries*, 1861, ser 2, v 11, 244
7 Baring-Gould, 77–8. Account from the Rev R. M. Heanley, Upton Grey Vicarage, Winchfield
8 Bell, 38
9 St Leger-Gordon, 171
10 *Choice Notes*, 17, 36–7, 114–15
11 Udal, 275, quoting *Dorset County Chronicle*, June 1888
12 Randell, 88–9
13 Bell, 35. Verjuice—sour juice of unripe apples, formerly used in cooking; a precursor of vinegar
14 Evans, *Pattern Under the Plough*, 176
15 *Berkshire Book*, 120 (the text referred to is Luke 16, 21); *Lancet* 1970, 1, 615, 848, 955; Bosworth Smith, R., *Bird Life and Bird Lore*, 1905, 360
16 Hartley, Dorothy, *Food in England*, 1954, 236
17 Marshall, 221
18 Dr David Speller; *British Medical Journal*, 1969, 3, 370
19 *Notes and Queries*, 1880, ser 6, v 1, 23
20 Pound, Louise, *Nebraska Folklore*, Lincoln, Nebraska, 1959, 29–30. Similar cures were widely known and practised through North American 'rattlesnake country'
21 *The Times*, 2 September 1972, 14
22 Whitney and Bullock, 83; Radford, 245
23 *Choice Notes*, 217
24 *Notes and Queries*, 1885, ser 6, v 11, 46
25 Brown, Theo, 'Charming in Devon', *Folklore*, Spring 1970, 81, 32–47
26 Radford, 56, 59–60
27 Coffin, Tristram P. and Cohen, Hennig, *Folklore in America*, New York 1966, 126, 238; Blakeborough, 141
28 Evans, *Pattern Under the Plough*, 84

29 *Choice Notes*, 249
30 Porter, 46
31 Porter, 10, 12
32 *Notes and Queries*, 1876, ser 5, v 5, 364
33 *Choice Notes*, 258
34 St Leger-Gordon, D., *Devonshire*, 1953, 274–5; St Leger-Gordon, Ruth E., *Dartmoor*, 137

Bibliography

Atkinson, J. C., *Forty Years in a Moorland Parish*, 1892

Aubrey, John, *Remaines of Gentilisme and Judaisme*, ed J. Britten, 1881

Baker, Margaret, *Discovering the Folklore of Plants*, Tring 1969

——, *Christmas Customs and Folklore*, Tring 1972

Baring-Gould, Sabine A., *A Book of Folk-Lore*, nd

Bell, Vicars, *To Meet Mr. Ellis*, 1956

Berkeley, M. and Jenkins, C. E., *A Worcestershire Book*, nd

The Berkshire Book: Compiled by Berkshire Federation of Women's Institutes, Reading 1951

Billson, C. J., *Leicestershire and Rutland. County Folklore: Printed Extracts: 3*, 1895

Blakeborough, R., *Wit, Character, Folk Lore and Customs of the North Riding of Yorkshire*, 1898

Botkin, B. A., ed, *A Treasury of New England Folklore*, New York 1965

Brand, John, *Observations on the Popular Antiquities of Great Britain*, arranged, revised and enlarged by Sir Henry Ellis, 1849, 3 v; 1877, 1 v

Burne, Charlotte, *Shropshire Folk-Lore*, 1883

——, *The Handbook of Folklore*, 1914

Canadian Folk-Lore, reprinted from *The Journal of American Folk-Lore*, 19 Lancaster, Pa, 1918, 31, nos 119–20

Chambers, R., ed, *The Book of Days, a Miscellany of Popular Antiquities*, 1862–4, 2v

Cheshire Village Memories; Being Extracts from Seventy-Four Scrapbooks of Local History Made by Members of the Women's Institutes, Malpas 1969

Choice Notes from 'Notes and Queries': Folk Lore, 1859

Coffin, Tristram P. and Cohen, Hennig, *Folklore in America*, New York 1966

Creighton, Helen, *Bluenose Magic: Popular Beliefs and Superstitions in Nova Scotia*, Toronto 1968

Bibliography

Cullum, Rev Sir John, *The History and Antiquities of Hawstead in the County of Suffolk*, 1784

Dacombe, Marianne R., ed, *Dorset Up Along and Down Along*, Dorchester 1951

Edwards, H., *A Collection of Old English Customs and Curious Bequests and Charities*, 1842

Evans, George Ewart, *Ask the Fellows Who Cut the Hay*, 1956

——, *The Horse in the Furrow*, 1960

——, *The Pattern Under the Plough: Aspects of the Folk Life of East Anglia*, 1966

Glyde, J., ed, *The Norfolk Garland*, 1872

——, ed, *The New Suffolk Garland*, 1866

Gurdon, Eveline Camilla, *Suffolk. County Folklore: Printed Extracts: 2*, 1893

Gutch, Mrs, *East Riding of Yorkshire. County Folklore: Printed Extracts: 8*, 1912

——, *Lincolnshire. County Folklore: Printed Extracts: 7*, 1908

——, *North Riding of Yorkshire, York and the Ainsty. County Folklore: Printed Extracts: 4*, 1901

Hand, Wayland, D., ed, *Popular Beliefs and Superstitions from North Carolina*, Durham, NC, 1964

Harland, John and Wilkinson, T. T., *Lancashire Folk-Lore*, 1867

Harman, H., *Buckinghamshire Dialect*, 1929, reprinted Wakefield 1970

Hartland, Edwin Sidney, *Gloucestershire. County Folklore: Printed Extracts: 1*, 1895

Henderson, William, *Notes on the Folk-Lore of the Northern Counties of England and The Borders*, 1866

Herrick, Robert, *Poems*, ed L. C. Martin, Oxford 1965

Hole, Christina, *English Custom and Usage*, 1942

Hone, William, ed, *The Table Book*, 1864

——, ed, *The Year Book*, 1864

——, ed, *The Every-Day Book*, 1826–7, 2 v

Hughes, Anne, *The Diary of a Farmer's Wife 1796–1797*, 1964

Hyatt, Henry Middleton, *Folk-Lore from Adams County, Illinois*, New York 1965

Jobson, Allan, *Under a Suffolk Sky*, 1964

Kilvert, Francis, *Diary 1870–1879; Selections*, ed William Plomer, 1944

Leather, E. M., *The Folk-Lore of Herefordshire*, 1912

Macaulay, Aulay, *The History and Antiquities of Claybrook in the County of Leicester*, 1791

Marshall, Sybil, *Fenland Chronicle*, Cambridge 1967

Bibliography

Misson de Valbourg, Henri, *Memoirs and Observations in His Travels Over England*, trans J. Ozell, 1719

Nicholson, John, *Folk-Lore of East Yorkshire*, 1890

Northall, C. F., *English Folk-Rhymes*, 1892

Porter, Enid, *Cambridgeshire Customs and Folklore*, 1969

Pound, Louise, *Nebraska Folklore*, Lincoln, Nebraska 1959

Radford, E. and M. A., *Encyclopaedia of Superstitions*, ed Christina Hole, 1961

Randell, Arthur R., *Sixty Years a Fenman*, ed E. Porter, 1966

Rose, Walter, *Good Neighbours*, Cambridge 1943

St Leger-Gordon, Ruth E., *The Witchcraft and Folklore of Dartmoor*, 1965, reprinted Wakefield 1972

Scot, Reginald, *Discoverie of Witchcraft*, 1584

Sternberg, Thomas, *Dialect and Folk-Lore of Northamptonshire*, 1851

Stout, Earl J., ed, *Folklore from Iowa*, New York 1936

Thomas, Daniel Lindsey and Lucy Blayney, *Kentucky Superstitions*, Princeton 1920

Tongue, Ruth L., *Somerset Folklore*, 1965

Tusser, Thomas, *Five Hundred Points of Good Husbandry*, 1573

Tyack, George S., *Lore and Legend of the English Church*, 1899

Udal, J. S., *Dorsetshire Folk-Lore*, 1922, reprinted Guernsey 1970

Whitney, Annie Weston and Bullock, Caroline Canfield, *Folk-Lore of Maryland*, New York 1925

Wolseley, Viscountess, *The Countryman's Log-Book*, 1921

Wright, Arthur R. and Lones, T. E., *British Calendar Customs: England*, 1936–40, 3 v

MANUSCRIPTS

Trump, A. M., 'Things My Grandmother Told Me'. Unpublished. This essay won the first prize for Devon in a competition organised by the Associated Countrywomen of the World, November 1938. Miss Trump's grandmother was born in 1831 and died in 1932. Until her marriage she lived at Clyst Hydon, Devon, one of a farmer's family of five girls and two boys. Miss Trump was born and brought up at Burrow Farm, Broad Clyst, and has a wide knowledge of Devon life. The Trump family has long connections with farming in the county.

Baker, Marion Cecilia, 'Memories of a Sussex Childhood 1894–1905'. Unpublished. Mrs Baker, now living in Buckinghamshire, was born in 1894 at Baldslow near Hastings, Sussex, where her father, Robert Aitken, was head

Bibliography

gardener at Beaulieu. Until the family moved to Rye in 1905, she lived at the East Lodge, one of seven children, four boys and three girls, all of whom keenly enjoyed country life.

English Dance and Song
Folklore (formerly *Folk-Lore*, formerly *Folk-Lore Journal*, formerly *Folk-Lore Record*)
Journal of American Folklore
Notes and Queries

Acknowledgements

I should like to thank Miss Christina Hole, Miss Enid Porter, Miss Ruth L. Tongue, Mrs Sybil Marshall, Dr Helen Creighton, Mr Arthur Randell, Mr Allan Jobson and others, who generously allowed me to draw upon their researches; Major J. Fairfax-Blakeborough permitted me to use his work and that of the late Mr Richard Blakeborough; Mrs Ruth E. St Leger-Gordon allowed me to refer both to her own work and to that of the late Mr D. St Leger-Gordon. My thanks are especially due to Miss A. M. Trump for her notes on Devon beliefs and for the use of her prize-winning essay 'Things My Grandmother Told Me', to my mother, Mrs M. C. Baker, for her informative recollections and for her essay 'Memories of a Sussex Childhood 1894–1905', to Dr David Speller of the University of Bristol for comments on 'Country Cures and Remedies' and to Mr and Mrs Cecil Atkins of Waddesdon for many helpful suggestions.

My thanks go also to: Mr Albert Van Citters, of The Empress Hotel, Victoria, British Columbia; Mrs E. Lahey, Lundy's Lane Historical Museum, Niagara Falls, Ontario; Miss J. M. Swann, Northampton Museum; Mr H. R. Bradley Smith, Shelburne Museum, Mr Richard Carter Barret, The Bennington Museum, Vermont, and Mr John Duffy, The Vermont Historical Society, Montpelier; Hampshire County Museum Service; The Pitt Rivers Museum, Oxford, and Mr Peter Narracott; The Director, Royal Botanic Gardens, Kew; The National Trust and Mr Lawrence Rich; Ottawa Public Library; Mr H. R. H. Harman, West Sussex County Library; Mrs Jean Williamson, Grosmont, Whitby and Mr Jack Scarth; Mrs Emmie

Acknowledgements

White, Northaw, Hertfordshire; Mrs Cecil C. Newcomb, Walton, Nova Scotia; Miss N. J. Quayle, Bury, Sussex; Mr Christopher D. Sansom, Godalming; Mr Alan Trump, Ledwell; Mr Duncan S. Gray and Mr O. F. Wills, Toronto; Ms Bernice Fuller, Traverse City Chamber of Commerce, Michigan; Mr F. Bennett, H. P. Bulmer Limited, Hereford; Mr Glenn E. Gavin, Liberal Chamber of Commerce, Kansas; Messrs Robert Hale and their authors for permission to refer to the *County Book* series; Liverpool University Press for permission to quote from *Blundell's Diary and Letter Book 1702–28*, ed M. Blundell; Oxford University Press for permission to quote from Professor L. C. Martin's edition of Robert Herrick's *Poems*; to readers of American and Canadian newspapers, *Country Life, Popular Gardening* and *Amateur Gardening* who sent me valuable information; and to Mrs Mary Farnell of Wendover, who skilfully prepared many of the photographs for the book and whose technical advice was of great value.

M.B.

Index

Index